Exploring Sound

creative musical projects for teachers

JUNE TILLMAN

LONDON:
STAINER & BELL

ACKNOWLEDGEMENTS

The publishers wish to thank the following for their permission to reproduce copyright material: Grete Fischer for the stories 'The Monkeys', 'The Weeds' and 'The Long Long Spoons' from her book *Stories for Argument*; Constable and Company Limited for the poem 'How goes the night' from *Lyrics from the Chinese*, translated by Helen Waddell; Doubleday and Company Inc. for the poem 'A trout leaps high' from *An Introduction to Haiku* by Harold G. Henderson; and Oxford and Cambridge University Presses for extracts from the New English Bible, Second Edition.

© 1976 Stainer & Bell Ltd
Reprinted 1985, 1995

ISBN 0 85249 310 X

Printed by Galliard (Printers) Ltd, Gt Yarmouth, Norfolk

CONTENTS

PREFACE

There are so many people who have helped me in this project that it is impossible to name them all. I should, however, like to mention the staff and pupils at Hogarth Junior Mixed School, Chiswick and Miss B. A. Double, the headmistress; at Burlington School, Shepherd's Bush and Mrs E. Moore, the headmistress; and at Thornhill Middle School, Southampton and Mr F. Watts, the headmaster. I am very grateful to Allen Percival, Bernard Braley, Marian Liebmann and David Evans for much help and encouragement, and to Grete Fischer for allowing me to use her stories in my work. Elizabeth Robinson managed a very difficult task in typing the original manuscript and Melvina Benyon helped a great deal in preparing the final version. My mother, Mrs N. Boyce, has given me much valuable support. Finally, I should like to thank my husband and young son for their tolerance and patience throughout the project.

June B. Tillman

CHAPTER 1
INTRODUCTION

Music is so often left out—of school timetables and school programmes, of integrated studies schemes. It is a fringe subject, the province of the specialist, the province of the cultivated few initiated into its mysteries. The musical gift is seen in terms of black and white—either you have it or you have not. (This has been less true of performance than of composition. 'At least everyone can sing' was the basis of many schemes of musical education.)

As long as this attitude persists the musical few in the classroom will be the odd ones, the different ones, perhaps even the 'cissy' ones, while the rest of the class will be denied musical experience. All children are expected to write, to draw, to paint: why not to make music? Not just singing in regimented rows, not just playing in the school percussion band or orchestra, not just listening in silence to records; but creating it, composing it. 'But,' say many teachers, 'I don't even play the piano!' It is not really necessary. 'I don't understand crotchets and quavers.' That is not really necessary. 'I can't sing in tune.' Even that isn't really necessary.

All of these things are, of course, a help, if used imaginatively and not only along the lines in which the subject called 'music' used to be taught. It is curious that in the visual arts most children are given paper and paint a long time before they are shown a Van Gogh masterpiece and many teachers teach art without being a Picasso. Some of the children's work will be far better than the teacher could ever produce. (He may even be teaching a budding Picasso.) By contrast, in music it has been deemed necessary to be thoroughly educated in musical masterpieces before one can even attempt to compose a tune. Is it not possible that everyone is capable of some musical utterance? Just as some children find self-expression easier in art than in words, there may be some who find that musical expression comes most naturally. Should we deprive them of the opportunity to express themselves in this way because they are not Beethovens? I have found that some children who show little imagination elsewhere can produce thoughtful musical work, and who am I to say that John's pattern on his drum is not an expression of his idea of rain falling, even if it is not what I should have done?

The traditional attitude to music may be due partly to the great stress laid on writing music down by means of sophisticated notational system, rather than on the sound of the composition itself. If you could not write it down, you could not compose. For this reason, the emphasis in the first chapter is on improvisation; only at a later stage will the children want to remember their work by writing it down. Traditional notation is used occasionally in this book, but I have also used other types of notation that are easy and straightforward, and new to everybody. A tape recorder, too, can often be used as a substitute for written notation; song tunes can be composed, recorded and learned by repetition (see chapter 2). Here there is no need to write anything down. What is needed primarily is sensitivity and imagination. The most important task is to give the children the opportunity and the material with which to achieve their potential.

There is a further point in favour of musical expression. The products of the musical activities described in chapter two are not only created by a group but also an expression of the group's feelings. An individual's work can be included in a group composition almost immediately. A more sophisticated method of group composition is the traditional blues (see page 27). This is a sequence of chords within which the group improvises. Given a pianist who is used to the sequence of chords or prepared to work at them, it is possible (for the older children) to compose blues, which also form a good background for the spoken word.

It is interesting to watch the way in which children, sometimes unconsciously and sometimes because of external pressure, will modify their original ideas to fit in with the group structure. This is most apparent when small groups are working together. The child who may start by creating a pattern and sticking to it regardless of other people, will later think about the musical effect of the whole group and modify his pattern to fit in with those of the others. At first, a child following on from another's melody may not take into account what has preceded him, but later he will begin to listen to the work of the previous person and even to pick up his rhythmic and melodic ideas and use them himself. The accent should always be on participation; every child should be included in each new project and, as far as possible, his contribution included in the final result. Group work is a valuable social exercise as well as a musical one.

Traditionally trained musicians may be tempted to despise the use of the term 'music' to describe the end products of such improvisatory beginnings, but in texture and general style they are not unlike the work of contemporary composers such as Varèse, Webern, Penderecki, John Cage, Charles Ives and composers using electronic techniques.

This book is not written primarily for the music specialist, but for the non-specialist who finds himself in any situation involving the teaching of children aged between about seven and fourteen; although older ones certainly enjoy this sort of music-making as well, and even younger ones will enjoy experimenting, although the more sophisticated organisation of compositions may be beyond them. A few links with other subjects have been indicated; but there is, in general, more literature about teaching them than there is about music. Technical language has been kept to a minimum. Although the book deals primarily with creating music, in my teaching I have always combined this with singing and listening, while some theoretical work arises quite naturally from it. The singing could well be accompanied by the children playing percussion parts rather than by the teacher on the piano or even the guitar. Listening to music on records seems much easier when it can be related to a subject that the class have already worked at creatively themselves. In choosing the records I have mentioned in the projects, I have tried to restrict myself to those most commonly found in school collections, for I prefer to spend my allowance on instruments rather than records.

All the teacher needs to do in a creative music-making lesson is to direct the children's ideas and help them to mould them into a class or group composition. This introductory chapter gives some idea of how such musical work can be used in the creation of an assembly with the whole class participating.

* * *

It was IIIB's turn for assembly again. What was it to be this time? One of the better readers stumbling through a parable or one of the more readable Old Testament stories? Or perhaps we could read some of our own stories? But then the people would be those who had read in assembly and provided the material for the past half year. 'Why can't we read in assembly?' is the cry of the others—but if the readings were to be audible and intelligible this was clearly impossible.

I thought of a subject we had been discussing recently: water. Could we not incorporate this in some way? We had examined it in science, religious education, history and geography. There were some good paintings—we could use these—and we had done some musical work. Couldn't we make our experience of water alive to the others through their ears as well as their eyes and brains?

So it came about that for that week thirty children grouped themselves on the stage. We set the mood for the rest of the school by playing a section from Britten's 'Sea Interludes' from *Peter Grimes,* a favourite from a variety of other people's musical ideas of water. Our own ideas followed on after this.

One scene was set by a group of girls who played a glissando on the glockenspiel to describe a forest glade, with a stream—suggested by gently rattling tambourine and triangle—flowing through it. This erupted into a waterfall described by a boys' group with lively rhythms on alto glockenspiel, open guitar strings, wood-blocks and rolling tambourine. We then returned to the town for subject matter, using gently shaken maracas to describe the water heating in a kettle; the sound was intensified by adding sandpaper blocks and a note blown across the top of a bottle until the climax of boiling occurred, portrayed by Indian cymbals and a teatray hit with a padded beater. A thirsty man in a desert searching for water was portrayed first on a rattle containing sand, later joined by another rattle containing peas shaken against a monotonous pattern on a wood-block. Chime bars described a flower opening and, with steady beats on flowerpots and glasses of water hit with the triangle beater, the rain fell. Deep in the sea—suggested by steady beats on a large tambour and patterns on a bass xylophone—a whale moved to rhythms from bongos with interpolations from a scraper. A sunny day by the seaside was suggested by claves, shakers, castanets and alto xylophone. The small waves rippled on the shingle (on scraper and glockenspiel) and gradually the rhythms combined and built up, with the addition of the wind (on a cymbal with wire brushes and a wobble-board), to a representation of a storm at sea.

Next we read the story of the stilling of the storm on the lake and we illustrated Psalm 93, accompanying the reading with a musical background. Here we thought about the majesty of God in relation to the sea. We used rhythms from the words of the psalms, choosing what we considered to be the chief word or phrase in each sentence and using the rhythm to accompany the following line, so that the final effect was:

Speaker	The Lord is king! He is clothed with majesty
Cymbal	𝅗𝅥 𝅗𝅥
Tambourine	
Speaking Chorus	majesty, majesty

8

Speaker — and covered with strength

Tambourine

Speaking Chorus — ma-je - sty   ma-je - sty, strength, strength

Cymbal

Speaker — Surely the earth is set firmly in place and cannot be moved

Cymbal

Speaking Chorus — strength   strength strength strength strength   cannot be moved, cannot be moved

Small tambour

Speaker — Your throne, Lord,   has been firm from the be-ginning,

Small Tambour

Speaking Chorus — Cannot be moved,   Cannot be moved,   be-ginning, be-ginning

Large Tambour

Speaker — and you existed   before time began

Large Tambour

Speaking Chorus — be-ginning,   be-ginning be-ginning time began time began

Triangle

Speaker — The ocean   depths raise their voice,   Lord.

Triangle

Speaking Chorus — time   be - gan   time   be - gan

Speaker — They raise their voice and roar

Wood-block

Speaker — Medi- ter-ra - ne - an   Medi- ter-ra - ne - an   Medi- ter-ra - ne - an

Bongo

Speaker — Caspi-an Cas-pi-an Caspi-an Caspi-an Caspi-an Cas-pi-an   Cas-pi-an

Shaker

Speaker — Sar- gas - so   Sar - gas-so   Sar - gas- so

Clapping

Speaker — Ad-ri - at - ic   Ad-ri - at - ic

Cymbal

Speaker — Dead

In this last section, to describe the noise of the sea we chose the rhythms of the names of the rivers and seas we had discovered on the map, for example: Mediterranean (♩♪♪♩ ♪♩.) Caspian (♩♪♪♩) and so on. We built them up, one by one, by name first; then each was transferred to whichever instrument seemed suitable.

During this assembly the concentration of both composers and listeners testified to the reality of the experience, and I felt that we had communicated our experience of the previous weeks in a new way. Because of our involvement, the rest of the school was caught up in it too.

CHAPTER 2
MUSICAL CREATION AND IMPROVISATION

THE EARLY STAGES

For music-making activities sit the children in a circle, which is the most suitable shape for this activity; the teacher sits as a member of this circle. Give an instrument to each child, trying to put different instrumental colours next to one another, so that each wooden-sounding instrument (such as wood-block, castanets or xylophone) is next to a metal instrument (such as triangle, Indian bell or glockenspiel). Skin instruments such as tambour, bongos or side drum should be contrasted with pottery or glass instruments such as flower pots or bottles. Try to see that there is an instrument for every child. It is very easy to make some simple instruments (see chapter 3), but if there are really not enough to go around, ask the children to use body sounds such as clapping, finger-snapping or blowing.

On a pitched instrument, it is difficult to produce a conventionally satisfying tune without a long period of experimentation or some theoretical knowledge. Some children may like the less conventional tunes produced by improvisation using all the available notes; but if the children want to produce more immediately satisfying tunes, it is a good idea to remove from instruments like glockenspiels and xylophones the 4th and 7th degrees of the major scale, leaving the five notes of the pentatonic scale CDEGAC (F and B having been removed). Chime bars may be distributed in combinations of three or four. For conventional sounds, give out combinations within a major scale (CDEFGAB), or common chords like CEG or DFA. For more unusual sounds, use any combination avoiding these; those using the augmented 4th (e.g. GAC♯), or chromatic steps (e.g. GF♯F♮) are particularly useful. The following description shows how one might set about a musical project describing water, such as the one in the opening chapter.

Ask each child to think about what water means to him, and how he might tell the person on his right about it musically. Allow a moment's thinking time, and then a moment's trial period. This can be ear-splitting; it is therefore better to use the school hall or a very large room, and to establish a visual stop signal rather than an oral one. The children should then play their ideas one by one while the others listen. Afterwards discuss the various ideas, and then set the children to work in pairs, fitting their ideas together. Next, focus their attention on describing the sea. Give each child a number—the smallest sounds first—and begin in order, signalling them to come in one by one, keeping their pattern going, and gradually building up the sound of a storm at sea. Try to fit every child's sound in somewhere, making sure that none is excluded.

Having tried this experiment once, discuss it together and suggest possible refinements that might be made. One child may feel his pattern or idea is more suitable for a different type of instrument; for example, a child to whom water suggests a very rapid rhythm may find this impossible to play on an instrument like a triangle, because the swing of the triangle to and fro makes rapid notes technically difficult. A child with a wood-block, which gives a light staccato tap, may feel strongly that his slower pattern needs a darker, more sustained tone colour—a large tambour would better achieve the effect that he has in mind. (When the children have more experience of this type of work, each child can choose his own instrument at the start of each session according to the tone colour he feels appropriate for the subject.) It may be that two children wish to fit their patterns together, and think that they sound better as a pair. Introducing the various sounds in pairs does shorten an otherwise lengthy piece, and may certainly help the teacher to remember the order of sound appearances more easily. For example, two children with bongos may have invented the same pattern and want to come in, and play, together. On the other hand, if their patterns happen to be the same, it may be desirable to pair one bongo player with long notes on a triangle and the second bongo player with a glissando from the glockenspiel. And, of course, some children may simply like the sound of their patterns together.

At this stage you may feel that the whole piece needs to be more, or less, rhythmic. At first, it is enough to keep a beat going with your hands, perhaps enlisting the aid of a drummer to keep it steady. But it may be that a child will protest that his pattern will not fit the beat and will be unwilling to modify it; or the class as a whole may feel that a subject such as the waterfall should not have a steady beat at all. In such cases one could have a non-metric section (without a steady beat) in which there were solos for the instruments with freer patterns, or the whole piece might be non-metric; although, in combining large numbers of patterns, this can lead to what sounds remarkably like total confusion!

When the whole appears to be nearly finished, you may find that new sounds suggest themselves, such as the sound of the wind added to the sea storm, and a gentle hissing to describe waves rippling on the shingle. Encourage the children to experiment with new sounds out of school and bring them to the next music-making session. By the next session, the class may well have learned more about storms in science or geography which may lead them to create a new musical composition, or you may want to use the storm as part of an illustration of a longer story, like the Stilling of the Tempest (Matthew 8). If, however, you feel that the composition is complete in itself, you might pursue another line of thought—perhaps one suggested by a child earlier in the project, such as the thirsty man in the desert, which may also link up with work in other subjects like geography.

The theme of thirst needs a more careful working out of the sequence of sounds than the storm: fewer simultaneous sounds in a more careful combination. Such a subject suggests a long first section in which the dryness, thirst, despair and longing can be portrayed. Instead of allowing each child to continue his sound indefinitely after making his entry, a better effect can be achieved here by using sounds for a limited time. Two or more different sounds can be combined in the same way as before; for example, a continuous shake of a maraca can be combined with isolated knocks on the wood-block and short shakes on a container full of peas to make up the opening sound. The sustained shake can be continued under the next group of sounds, which might show the longing for water, suggested by glissandi on a glockenspiel and complementary patterns on two triangles and a pair of Indian cymbals. The thirsty man's despair might also contain the maraca roll, but now combined with isolated beats from two tambours—one high, one low. Such complex combinations will involve a great deal of discussion and experimentation.

LATER DEVELOPMENTS

As the children become used to these ideas, they can take over from the teacher the role of organising the activity. It is often easier for them to work in smaller groups than to manage the whole class, and this brings more freedom to the session. The children can choose their own instruments at the start. In a project I worked on, a group describing spring chose all metallic-sounding instruments such as glockenspiels, triangles and cymbals; the group describing winter, skin and wood sounds such as xylophones and drums. The 'spring' group added to their sounds some pins shaken in a tin, and a collection of thin metal strips suspended from a wooden bar, which could be shaken. Try to have readily available a collection of materials for making instruments, so that children can produce new sounds as they need them (see chapter 3). This activity may well spill into break periods as well.

At this stage, the children will probably want to write down their work, but it is seldom possible to use conventional notation. A set of boys I taught had great problems in writing down a composition built entirely of sounds obtained from a metal-framed stool. Three players were involved. One hit the leather-padded top with a skipping rope; another worked out a pattern with a skittle on the rungs of the steel tubing between the legs (which were of different pitches because the legs tapered towards the top); the third dropped bean-bags at periodic intervals. They opted for an extremely simple notation:

We worked at a more complex notation which could be used for the thirsty man in the desert:

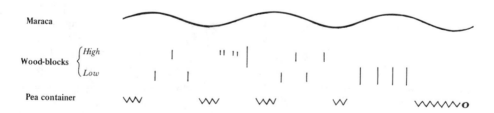

Here, there is more indication of time lengths by the spacing of the wood-block taps; high and low pitches were used, and the length of stroke indicates the loudness. The undulating maraca line means a lazy roll, and the jagged pea-container line represents a more violent continual shake, the final O representing one shake only. The final composition still contains a large element of improvisation, which is aided by the fact that the composer is generally the performer! (George Self's notation in *New Sounds in Class,* published by Universal Edition, is useful here.)

In the initial stages of such a music project, some quick shorthand is needed to work out and remember the various sounds in their proper order. The one I use consists of a circle of dashes, each dash representing a child. The first time round, I mark S (small),

M (medium) and L (large), according to volume level, and then number them in the order they are to occur, so that it looks like this:

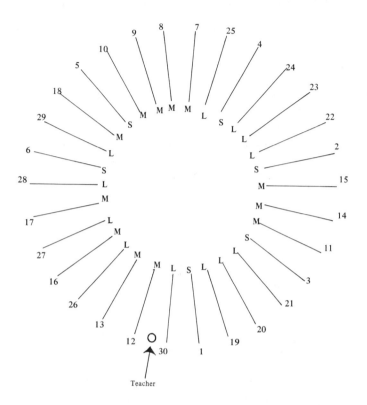

Teacher

From the beginning the children have to make some effort at remembering their own number and take some responsibility for making their entry at the right time. A clock can be useful in helping them to organise their sounds, noting down how many seconds each sound is to last.

At this stage, the children can also start to sort out for themselves which notes they require on the pitched instruments, although they may need some help here (see p. 10). They also begin to want real tunes rather than patterns and are prepared to spend a long time experimenting with a variety of notes. They may try to incorporate tunes they already know into their work, and to combine tunes, although here they will run into problems. They may have a desire for experimental effects: for instance, the 'spring' group mentioned previously might want to divide the tune between their pitched instruments on the basis of 'one note for you, one note for me' (which will give an effect similar to Webern's scoring).

Longer stories can now be attempted as a class project, each group dealing with a separate part. For example, in the story *The Long Long Spoons* described in Project 14 (p. 94) a group should be assigned to work on each of the eight musical pieces.

It helps the children to become more involved with their topic if they listen to music related to it. On the topic of water, the following works are useful: Debussy—'En Bateau' from *Petite Suite,* and *La Mer*; Britten—'Sea Interludes' from *Peter Grimes*; Mendelssohn—*Fingal's Cave*; Elgar—Variation 13 of *Enigma Variations*; and

Walton—*Portsmouth Point*. Sea shanties also help to bring the seaman's world, with its hardships and changes, alive (a suitable record is Topic TOP98: Blow the Man Down; this should be introduced carefully, for children not used to traditional singers may find the rough singing style strange).

EXTENSIONS OF SOUND PATTERN TECHNIQUES

The children will be able to suggest a variety of new techniques as the topic gets under way. Some useful ideas are listed below.

Word Rhythms Some children have problems in creating a consistent rhythm pattern which they can maintain in a composition like a storm. Repeating words can be helpful here, particularly those associated with the subject in some way; for example, for a storm: furiously (♫ ♩ ♪), tumultously (♪ ♫ ♪), raging (♩ ♪). The word rhythms can then be transferred to an instrument and used in the large sound picture. The whole of an abstract picture can be based on rhythms of words associated with it. The sea in Psalm 93 in chapter 1 is a good example of this. An effective picture of the speed of urban life can be created from the names of underground stations. Piccadilly Circus (♫♫ ♩ ♪), Notting Hill Gate (♫ ♩ ♪), Bank (♩), Bond Street (♩ ♪), Marble Arch (♫ ♪), Lancaster Gate (♫♩ ♪) and High Street Kensington (♩ ♩ ♫ ♪), built up slowly on top of one another with or without instruments, give a very hectic impression!

In illustrating a poem this technique of word rhythms can be used to highlight important words (see the treatment of Psalm 93 in the introduction), which naturally leads to a discussion of which *are* the most important words. One class I worked with applied this idea to William Blake's 'The Tyger':

> Tyger! Tyger! burning bright
> In the forests of the night,
> What immortal hand or eye
> Could frame thy fearful symmetry?

They thought that a combination of rhythms in the first line was necessary and decided that the tone colours of the cymbal and tambourine were most suitable. So the first line was introduced by the rhythm of the Tyger (♩ ♪) and accompanied by 'burning bright' (♫ ♩):

This accompaniment was continued through the second line since the children thought it had the same atmosphere as the first one. In the third line, 'immortal'

(♪ ♫) was singled out and the tone colour of the tambour was considered appropriate. So it ran:

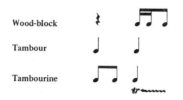

Then, having accompanied the fourth line in a similar way, they emphasised the 'fearful symmetry' with this rhythm (♫ ♫♪) as the verse finished:

Wood-block	
Tambour	
Tambourine	

Even though the word pattern is being transferred to an instrument, the significance of the rhythm will remain for the class if not for the listener.

Word Colours   Words have a 'colour' as well as a rhythm. Words with a bright 'a' sound (as in *rat)* may sound happy (*pat, ratatat, glad-handler, gathering, garlanded*), while those containing 'oo' may suggest unrest, discontent or darkness (*gloomy, feverfew, smooth, hooded*). Words like *gateway, away, lazy, railway, fading, jay* and *flail* may suggest relaxation; while those like *raw, flawless, mauling, pawpaw* and *awesome* may be considered to have an empty bleak sound.* Encourage the children to say them in such a way that the syllable with important 'colour' is emphasised.

Children also enjoy making up pieces (often comic) from isolated sounds they can make with their voices and mouths. It is even more fun writing them down and getting other people to perform them. This is an example of one composed by an eleven-year-old girl:

Instrumental Colours   Instruments can be used almost arhythmically simply for their tone colours. Into this category come such sounds as scratching sandpaper over the surface of a drum; making a stirring sound on flowerpots by rubbing a triangle beater round the edge; producing a tremolo on a chime bar by rubbing a strip of card backwards and forwards over the sound-hole while it is sounding. With experience and encouragement the children listen for and invent what are often very carefully prepared tone colours.

The link between instrumental colour and visual colour is one that has fascinated

* Such associations are purely subjective, but they do provide a starting point for the children's imagination.

musicians. In Arthur Bliss's *Colour Symphony* each movement has a colour for its title. Walt Disney's film *Fantasia* provides a further starting point for discussion with its attempts to transfer music into visual patterns. Orchestral instruments or perhaps instrumental families are often described as having a 'colour', although it is easier for children to stay with the simpler percussion instruments for their own work. They can still enjoy making up a complete 'colour suite'. Like Arthur Bliss, who studied heraldry before writing the *Colour Symphony*, they may find it easier if they associate a colour with a particular mood, an obvious one being the association of blue with sky and sea.

Body Sounds   Even without any instruments a child can produce a variety of sounds using his body alone. These include clapping (in a variety of ways: flat-handed, cup-handed, with two fingers), whistling, humming, stamping, finger-snapping and so forth. This can be linked with the experiments in notation mentioned under the heading 'Word Colours' (see p. 15).

Polyrhythm   This is the simultaneous combination of conflicting rhythm patterns. It is often quite hard to maintain these patterns one against the other. The easiest polyrhythmic pattern to start with is a division of the beat into two, set against its division into three. This also highlights the distinction between simple and compound time. Simple time like $\frac{2}{4}$ has a beat (♩) that will divide by two (♫); compound time like $\frac{6}{8}$ has a beat (♩.) that will divide by three (♫♪). Here is a polyrhythmic pattern using this distinction.

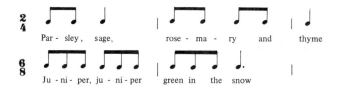

The subject is most easily approached using the rhythms of words and is often quite a natural result of the rhythmic word pictures discussed at the beginning of this chapter (see also Project 9 on p. 74).

BUILDING UP A COMPOSITION

Sometimes children's compositions seem to lack unity. (This may, however, seem so only to ears conditioned by Western music, and not to the children's ears; so be careful throughout this kind of work not to impose too many of your own ideas on them.) When the children themselves begin to realise and comment on the formlessness, that is the time to start teaching the elements of musical form.

The simplest form to introduce is the one in which the first section or first sound recurs at the end, after a middle section of contrasting material. In the world of musical terminology this rejoices in the name of *ternary* form. Thus, in a sequence on fire, for example, one might start off with a collection of instruments that suggest the smoke, then lead into those that may be associated with the flames, returning to the smoke music at the end.

An extension of ternary form is *rondo* form, in which the first section recurs several times throughout the piece, with contrasting material in between. This gives the pattern ABACA. This is particularly useful if one child's or one group's contribution is particularly good, when it can be used as the A material joining the other children's contributions. For example, one class of mine built up a 'space rondo' using words and instruments. The word 'space', with its suggestion of vastness and mystery, was accompanied on glockenspiel and cymbal and used as the main theme. The first contrasted section (sometimes called an *episode*) was Mercury and Neptune—light and airy-sounding words accompanied by triangles, Indian cymbals, bells and maracas. The second was Mars and Pluto—heavy and solid, with drums and scrapers. So the overall plan looked like this:

A	Space	glockenspiel and cymbal
B	{ Mercury	triangles, Indian cymbals
	{ Neptune	bells, maracas
A	Space	glockenspiel and cymbal
C	{ Mars	drums
	{ Pluto	scrapers
A	Space	glockenspiel and cymbal

Variation form is one of the oldest forms of instrumental music. In this form, a tune is first heard and is then changed or decorated or developed (varied) as the piece progresses. The art of decorating a melody by adding a lot of extra notes (as Mozart often does in his variations, or as Handel does in the famous variations called 'The Harmonious Blacksmith') is not an easy task for someone who is not very skilled at playing a melodic instrument; and it is only slightly easier to do it vocally. A tune can, however, be varied quite easily by playing it on a different instrument, or with different accompanying instruments, playing it on more instruments at a time, or playing it louder or softer, higher or lower, faster or slower. Changing into different time signatures is fun. A tune that started as a jig:

might become a march:

or a waltz:

or a Latin American tango:

Children can come upon such variation techniques by chance: for example, by playing a tune in the 'wrong' rhythm. Britten's popular *Young Person's Guide to the Orchestra* shows very clearly how a theme can be transferred to various instruments. If one listens to the commentary as well, the difference between the way in which each instrument plays the tune is also highlighted. Teachers who wish to pursue these ideas further will find many examples in classical music and in any book on musical form.

These three forms all suppose that a composition will be of some length. For shorter compositions the *ostinato* rhythm or melody is a useful technique. This is a melodic or rhythmic pattern that can be repeated over and over again underneath, while changing patterns are played above it. It is a quick and easy way to unify a diffuse piece. A very simple ostinato composed of two notes a fifth apart—for example, C and G played in steady crotchets on a xylophone or on the bass of the piano will fit with almost anything. It is particularly effective with a march-like piece.

For vocal or instrumental improvisations the ostinato is kept going by one player while two others improvise a conversation about it. This is a fragment of song from Project 14 (see p. 94).

It looks very complicated written down, but is in fact very simple to compose by ear. The children will probably invent longer and more complicated ostinati, but make sure that the pattern is not too complicated or too difficult to be repeated steadily.

A rhythmic ostinato can often be derived from the words of a poem (a technique already shown many times; see pp. 7, 14). The following traditional jingle is unified by the strong rhythmic pattern of its lines:

> Don't care didn't care,
> Don't care was wild.
> Don't care stole plum and pear
> Like any beggar's child.
>
> Don't care was made to care,
> Don't care was hung;
> Don't care was put in a pot
> And boiled till he was done.

However, it could well be accompanied by:

throughout. (An instrumental piece could be built up around this ostinato rhythm, perhaps using some of the rhythms from the rest of the poem as well.)

The piano keyboard has a wide range and all ten fingers are used to play it. This means that an effective piano piece can be built up around a single pattern which lies under the fingers of one hand:

This can be repeated high and low, loud and soft, on white or black notes and so forth. Variety might be provided by doing different things with the other hand; or if this is too difficult, accompanying the piece with various other instruments (see Project 6, p. 62).

A piano pattern may be created around a chord—that is, any collection of notes sounding at the same time. (In fact, if you hold the right-hand pedal down while playing the pattern above, this becomes a chord.) A common chordal pattern easily played on the piano is this:

This chord (called a *triad*) has formed the basis of the method of combining tunes and accompaniments in Western music for some 400 years. Composers working at the keyboard have often used these chords as the basis of their accompaniments.

There are, however, other chords available, and time spent in experimenting will reveal many interesting and unusual possibilities such as:

Such a chord can form the basis of a whole piece. Pitched instruments like chime bars may play it underneath the main melody in a simple rhythmic pattern:

A further melodic instrument can improvise a tune around it:

Further ideas about this subject can be found in Project 6 on p. 62.

If a piece is built around the notes of a chord, whether it be a common triad or a more unusual chord, any melody created will work in canon with itself. That is, a second voice starting at any time after the first voice can sing the same tune and it will fit. The beautiful Jewish round 'Shalom, my friends' is an example of one based around a D minor chord (DFA):

A very simple example made up by one class of 8-year-olds, based round the triad of C major (CEG), is:

The other voices can start anywhere and the parts will fit together perfectly.

A composition can be organised around a particular dynamic pattern. A crescendo (gradually getting louder) is the commonest one used, for it results naturally from using the smallest sounds first and then gradually adding the larger sounds. (Ravel's *Bolero* and Grieg's 'In the Hall of the Mountain King' are two examples of pieces that illustrate this.) Other dynamic patterns are also possible. The Walt Whitman passage (p. 69) might inspire a piece built around the recurring dynamic pattern of the sea's rise and fall:

<> <> <>

Silence is such a rapidly vanishing commodity in contemporary society that it might be a good idea to build a whole piece around it. Here a clock is useful for telling the children how long to wait before bringing in the next sound, although the intervals can be judged by the class or indicated by the conductor. A class has to gradually become used to the idea of silence, as it may be quite frightening for them. But it can be very exciting when small sounds are inserted into pockets of silence (see Project 11 on p. 79).

A composition can also be organised around sounds of a particular character or made by one kind of material or even one particular instrument. For example, the Jeremy Taylor passage (p. 56) uses cymbal sounds while 'Autumn' (p. 79) uses rustling and maraca sounds. Compositions organised in this way usually need contrasted rhythms and themes; otherwise, with one tone-colour, they may become boring.

The use of numbers in organising compositions is a method gaining increasing popularity with contemporary composers. (Tristram Cary's '3 4 5' (Stainer and Bell) is but one example.) In this case, work in the music lesson may be related to that in mathematics, as various number properties, such as square numbers and triangular numbers are explored. Here is a very simple example of a piece one class built around the number 24, the factors of which are 2, 3 and 4. The chime bar ostinato continues throughout, lasting 24 beats in all, and is largely made up of notes 2, 3 and 4 crotchets long.

This caused the rhythm to be a mixture of $\frac{2}{4}$, $\frac{3}{4}$ and $\frac{4}{4}$ (two, three and four crotchet beats in a bar respectively). At first this was emphasised by a triangle, drum and wood-block playing as follows:

Tambourine

Wood-block

Drum

After that the possibilities were endless. A maraca played for 24 beats and was silent for 24. Later, patterns of beats divided into 2, 3 and 4 were played simultaneously (see note on polyrhythm, p. 16):

In all each instrument entered 24 times, and the chime bar ostinato occurred 24 times. A canon was worked out with the parts having a pattern based on a beat divided into 2, 3 and 4. The second part entered two notes after the first, and the third, four notes after the second:

Wood-block

Drum

Tambourine

The more mathematical children were very interested in this (as they always have been interested in musical notation), although there were considerable difficulties in performance.

Melodic Attempts

The problems of creating a melody in a class teaching situation are not to be under-estimated. One should not ask the children to actually write a melody down for a very long time, for this immediately shackles their imagination, and their ideas disappear while they stumble over the first crotchet or quaver; however, the teacher may write them down or record them on tape. But one must not expect polished eight-bar long melodies neatly finishing on the doh of the key.

When one first attempts a longer musical composition including the use of speech, one meets the further problem of relating melody to words. One can place the speech against an ostinato background (see p. 18), using different instruments and rhythms to accompany each character. In Project 14 (p. 94), for example, one class decided that a triangle and Indian cymbal were right for Ali, whom they thought to be rather bewildered. The imposing guardian was accompanied by a slower pattern on a tambour and a large cymbal with padded stick.

Alternatively, when there is a suitable atmosphere in the class the pupils can improvise a melody for the words freely (rather like traditional recitative, or the example quoted in the section about ostinati on p. 18). This often works better with younger children or children who have been improvising vocally since they were young. When the composition has been repeated a number of times, this improvisation tends to codify into a melody quite naturally without any conscious effort having been made to create one.

The idea of holding a conversation vocally can be transferred to instruments; children who are too inhibited to improvise vocally will find this much easier. Use a pair of glockenspiels or recorders improvising over a bass xylophone or piano ostinato as described on p. 18. You can leave only the pentatonic scale on the melodic instruments (see pp. 10 and 24-25). Gradually each child will begin to listen to the other's melody and relate his own to it.

More conventional instruments (for example, piano or orchestral instruments) are useful for playing ostinati, particularly the lower pitched instruments. They can also be usefully introduced if improvisations codify into melodies. If, however, inexperienced players are attempting to improvise on these instruments, the danger is that they will be too concerned with the technical demands of the instrument to improvise freely. Because of this, simpler percussion instruments may be more appropriate for free improvisations.

One simple device that may be introduced into these conversations is the repetition of a phrase or motif slightly higher or lower in pitch. It is one way of picking up what the previous person has said in a conversation or varying the tune. For example:

Many folk tunes make use of this device in their construction such as, 'Polly put the kettle on':

Two more sophisticated techniques that might be used are inversion (upside-down) and retrograde (back-to-front) versions of a tune. A melody may be inverted by making the notes go up where the original notes went down and vice versa (see Project 7 on p. 67). So:

becomes;

This is like a mirror version. It requires a degree of musical expertise to be able to do this in improvisations. It could, however, be done only approximately, and more exact inversion might be used only in more organised composition.

The use of the retrograde version (using the tune or rhythm back to front) is even more complicated and may need working out more carefully. Thus:

becomes:

Composing songs, rather than merely improvising tunes, can be approached in a variety of ways. Some of these are related to improvised song (since all melody starts as improvisation) and also to chant. Some poems have a mysterious atmosphere that will allow a chant on one note, accompanied by curious and unusual sounds. This old Scottish poem by Murdoch Maclean has an atmosphere of mystery that lends itself perfectly to this treatment:

> Trim the cruisie's* failing light,
> The Son of God shall pass this night,
> Shall pass at midnight dreary,
> The Son of Mary weary.
>
> Lift the sneck† and wooden bar
> And leave the stranger's door ajar,
> Lest He may tarry lowly,
> The Son of Mary holy.
>
> Sweep the hearth and pile the peat,
> And set the board‡ with bread and meat;
> The Son of God may take it,
> The son of Mary break it.

A mysterious, sinuous tune could be played on a pair of recorders or glockenspiels accompanied by unpitched percussion:

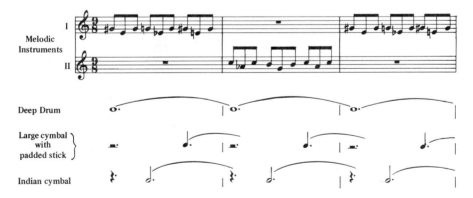

It is a short step from chanting on a single note to the sort of three-note chanting that characterises folk songs like skipping and counting-out rhymes. It is easiest to do with strongly rhythmic poems like:

> There was a monkey climbed up a tree;
> When he fell down, then down fell he.

*lamp   † latch   ‡ table

There was a crow sat on a stone;
When he was gone, then there was none

There was an old wife did eat an apple;
When she'd eat two, she'd eat a couple.

There was a horse a-going to the mill;
When he went on, he stood not still.

There was a butcher cut his thumb;
When it did bleed, the blood did come.

There was a lackey ran a race;
When he ran fast, he ran apace.

There was a cobbler mending shoon*;
When they were mended, they were done.

There was a chandler making candle;
When he them strip, he did them handle.

There was a navy went to Spain;
When it returned, it came again.

If the children recite this rhythmically it will gradually form itself into a tune. It was possibly in this way that a simple response song like 'Shout for Joy' began:

Another way of starting is by taking a limited range for the tune. Ask the children to take a range of, say, four notes and sing them over; these four notes should be the range of their tune. An example of this can be seen in the setting of Shelley's 'Dirge' (p. 64). It works well with sad poems like the 'Dirge' and also with rhythmic ones like those suggested for chanting.

The pentatonic scale has already been mentioned (see p. 10) as a suitable one for 'beginner melody writers'. It is the major scale without its 4th and 7th degrees: GABDEG (C and F♯ are missing). It is also the pattern of the black notes of the piano.

* shoes

Many folk melodies are based on this scale, like 'Amazing Grace':

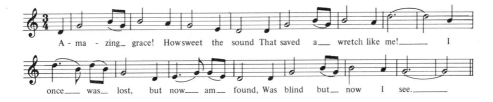

A - ma - zing_ grace! How sweet the sound That saved a__ wretch like me!_____ I

once__ was__ lost, but now__ am__ found, Was blind but__ now I see._____

Pentatonic melodies have a distinctive flavour that often gives them a rather wistful, haunting quality. As a tune for a ballad like Charles Kingsley's 'The Sands of Dee' it is an ideal scale:

'O Mary, go and call the cattle home,
　And call the cattle home,
　And call the cattle home
　Across the sands of Dee;
The western wind was wild and dank with foam,
　And all alone went she.

The western tide crept up along the sand,
　And o'er and o'er the sand,
　And round and round the sand,
　As far as eye could see.
The rolling mist came down and hid the land:
　And never home came she.

'O! is it weed, or fish, or floating hair—
　A tress of golden hair,
　A drownèd maiden's hair,
　Above the nets at sea?
Was never salmon yet that shone so fair
　Among the stakes on Dee'.

They rowed her in across the rolling foam,
　The cruel crawling foam,
　The cruel hungry foam,
　To her grave beside the sea:
But still the boatmen hear her call the cattle home
　Across the sands of Dee.

Poems set to a pentatonic tune can be accompanied with melodic ostinati based on the pentatonic scale, for the scale will work, however it is used, as a counter-tune to itself. (Both tune and counter-tune must, however, use the scale starting on the same note. A tune using the pentatonic scale starting on G will not fit with one based on the black notes of the piano.)

Another method is to take a chord sequence and play it over on guitar or piano or chime bars, repeating it in a set rhythmic pattern. The class can then improvise tunes around it. A simple sequence with an interesting flavour is E minor (EGB) to D major (DF♯A). It can be arranged on chime bars quite simply and a tune hummed above it:

An extension of this sequence is a common one in more recent compositions in 'folk' style: E minor (EGB), D major (DF#A), C major (CEG), B major (BD#F#). A comic song based on this runs:

Poems with shorter lines lend themselves well to this treatment, and this example by fifteen-year-old Caroline Broadhurst is based on a sequence similar to the one above. Both words and music are by her and it is interesting to note how the tune gets more complicated as the verses proceed:

Her piano part is repeated all the way through, modified only in the half-speed version shown at the end of the song, and contains a right-hand part made up entirely of an ostinato pattern (see p. 18). This is only the first of four verses.

The blues sequence G G7 C D7 is a good one that has formed the basis of many songs that have started as improvisations. (Those who wish to study the blues further could consult *The Art of Folk Blues Guitar* by Jerry Silverman (Oak Publications), which deals with the chord sequences and finger styles; or *The Story of the Blues* by Paul Oliver (Hanover Books), which is more concerned with the history.) The blues is perhaps the most developed form using this method of composition.

Many other sequences can be discovered by experimenting. A poem of the type that would suit this technique well—using the somewhat unusual sequence of E major

(EG♯B), A minor (ACE), E major (EG♯B), C major (CEG)—is the anonymous poem
that follows:

> I sing of a mayden
> That is makéless.[1]
> King of all kings
> To her son she ches[2].
> He came al so stille
> Where his moder[3] was,
> As dew in Aprille
> That falleth on the grass.
> He came al so stille
> To his moder's bow'r,
> As dew in Aprille
> That falleth on the flow'r.
> He came al so stille
> Where his moder lay,
> As dew in Aprille
> That falleth on the spray.
> Moder and mayden
> Was never none but she;
> Well may such a lady
> Goddés[4] moder be.

For this the accompanying chords could be arranged less severely, for example:

Melodic Shapes

This is dealt with more fully in Project 6 in relation to ice patterns (p. 63). Tunes
have a shape which can be brought out by drawing a line joining the note heads. Thus,
the opening of the first song of Schubert's *Winter Journey* is a drooping tune:

Beethoven's piano sonata Op. 10 No. 1 opens with a jagged theme, in rhythm as well as
melodic shape:

while his first sonata in F minor starts with a theme that rises steadily up:

[1] matchless   [2] chose   [3] mother   [4] God's

In Mendelssohn's 'Hebrides Overture' the upward curve is perhaps intended to represent the soaring columns of Fingal's Cave:

The opening of 'Morning' from Grieg's *Peer Gynt* suite undulates gently within a compass of six notes:

Disjointed and angular, with wide jumps, is the broom's theme from *The Sorcerer's Apprentice* by Dukas:

There are circular tunes that wind round and round upon themselves, like that of Chopin's Waltz Op. 64 No. 1 (often called the 'Minute Waltz'):

An investigation of Kenneth Payne's *Tonescripts* will show this technique worked out more fully in relation to orchestral scores. They can be obtained from Star College, 19 Crawford Road, London SE 5. Creating a tune of a specified shape can be the starting point for melody invention, and can be linked with art work.

Music and Words

The ways in which music and words can be most effectively combined is a subject that has occupied many of the significant men in musical history—Monteverdi, Gluck, Wagner, Liszt and Strauss, to name but a few. Most of the examples of worked-out projects in this book have been based on poetry or poetic prose of some kind. Sometimes there are indications of how to create a tune for the words and turn the poem into a song, with suggestions for a varied accompaniment, or, more often, just for atmospheric instrumental effects. It is possible to speak the poem leaving gaps for the effects, but this tends to break up the sense and rhythm of the poem too much, unless the musical effects are added only between distinct verses. The musical effects may proceed simultaneously with the reading, but in this case care has to be taken that one does not obliterate the other. The music can be tape recorded and the volume adjusted to the speaking voice in performance; or if there is access to a tape recorder with a device for superimposing sound onto a tape already recorded, the whole can be tape recorded. (This latter is very difficult unless the tape recorder is also fitted with ear-phones which enable one to listen to the sound balance as the superimposition takes place.) But by far the most effective way is to use the poem as a prelude to the music, or vice versa. The musical sounds then do not necessarily have to adhere slavishly to the order in the poem and can be organised along lines that seem musically sensible (these have already been discussed in this chapter). The poem will then be the stimulus for the musical sounds, and in atmosphere the poem and the music are still related.

There is no reason why all the suggested sounds and sound explorations should not be pursued as sounds in their own right, without the addition of poetry or prose or indeed any external stimulus. There are many teachers and pupils who may prefer it this way; methods of building sounds up and combining them have been discussed already in this chapter. In this book words are used as a stimulus for the creation of musical sounds, which may constitute an easier approach for the non-musician. After the ideas have come they can be organised as purely musical sounds, forgetting their original inspiration. People with musical training may find the use of words unnecessary and unhelpful; they can set about these explorations in other ways.

Incidental music for dramatic activity differs in that the stimulus for its composition is before the eyes of the listener while he is actually hearing the music. This piece of prose by 12-year-old Anthony Duhaney entitled 'Fear' could be taken as the basis for a dramatic scene:

The moon reflected shadows on the dingy black water. It was a dull scenery and motionless. Then suddenly through green crunchy leaves eyes glittered like jewels. Their slithery scales mingled brown and green. Their eyes glaring, death, death. Their eyes glaring death and intent to kill. Their white fangs desperate to dig into human flesh. Then slithery figures slid into the black water. My heart began to beat fainter, beating with fear. Sweat dribbled down my crumpled face.

The opening of this could inspire a composition mingling dull wooden sounds and bright metallic ones, but the spirit of the piece might be even better captured if some thought were given to the way in which a tense atmosphere can be created in music as it has been by the words in the passage. One might start with small sounds widely spaced (rather like the night music on p. 50) and gradually make them bigger and closer together; or perhaps very low sounds ranging slowly up to high sounds; or a changing pattern of sounds held together by a drum beat, first soft, then relentlessly becoming louder; or an ostinato rhythm gradually becoming louder. (This can be compared with 'Mars' from Holst's suite *The Planets,* in which the same rhythm is repeated throughout. The rhythmically asymmetric repeated chords in this piece might also be discussed as a way of creating a climax.) The class might also listen closely to the ways in which a tense atmosphere is created on both radio and television, afterwards holding a discussion about the ways in which these two media differ.

Stereophonic effects

Writers of contemporary music are rediscovering the various effects that can be obtained by placing groups of instruments or voices at some distance apart from one another. (The composers of choral music at the turn of the seventeenth century exploited the musical effect of having several choirs in different galleries of a church answering one another across the building.) Many interesting effects can be obtained by placing groups of children in different corners of the hall, so that they can hold a musical conversation across an open space (see pp. 70 and 91). The children will be fascinated by the effect of the sound moving. Stand the children in a circle and tell them to hum only when the teacher points a finger at them; as the teacher stands in the centre of the circle, slowly rotating, they will be able to hear the sound 'move'. There is no good reason why musical compositions should always be performed by people standing as close to one another as possible. The more people involved, the more difficult this becomes; so why should we not use this difficulty to advantage and space groups apart?

Using a tape recorder

In this kind of work a tape recorder can be an invaluable asset. It saves having to write children's compositions down quickly in order to remember them. It is by far the best way of keeping these compositions because it emphasises the fact that the most important aspect is the sound, not precise symbols on a written page. (The written page is important here only if another group tries to perform the composition working from the composers' symbols—a very interesting exercise.) The children may also be more inclined to polish a performance for a recording; and it will help them to assess their work and comment constructively on it. It is difficult for children to comment on a composition in which they are actually taking part. It will also impress upon them the need to change instruments quietly and keep unwanted instruments still.

If two tape recorders are available they can be linked by a lead running from the output socket of one to the intake socket of the other, and some interesting effects can be obtained by changing the speed of the tapes. An ordinary word spoken at normal level and recorded at $7\frac{1}{2}$ i.p.s. will come out as a lion roaring at $1\frac{7}{8}$ i.p.s.; speech recorded at $1\frac{7}{8}$ i.p.s. will come out like the chatter of a budgerigar at $7\frac{1}{2}$ i.p.s.

The tape can be played at the new speed on one machine and recorded onto a new tape in the required place. It is sometimes difficult to get the sounds in the desired order on the main tape. For this, editing may be necessary; an editing block, a sharp pair of scissors and some editing tape will be required. The particular sound is literally cut out of the tape with a diagonal cut and stuck into the required place on the shiny side of the main tape. It is not beyond the capacity of intelligent 10-year-olds to master these tricks of tape recording. At least one school I know issues its pupils with tape recording badges when they have passed a proficiency test.

On tape recorders instrumental sounds can be changed beyond all recognition, which means that these techniques can produce a range of sounds comparable to those of the BBC's Radiophonic Workshop, which produces incidental music for its films, especially its space and horror ones. The children will probably find it much easier to listen to electronic music after having tried their hand at such composition themselves.

CHAPTER 3

MUSICAL INSTRUMENTS

It is a good idea to have as great a variety of sound colours as possible available, in contrast to the old idea of a percussion band with, for example, a number of tambourines, triangles or drums playing simultaneously. For this reason the instruments in this chapter are arranged according to the material from which they are made; which, of course, largely dictates what sort of sound they will make, and also the length of time a note made on the instrument will last. In general, metal instruments have greater sustaining power than wooden ones, while that of skin-covered instruments like drums depends on their size and quality. The shaken instruments can produce a sustained sound when given a continuous shake (this is represented in the chapters of this book either by ∿∿∿ , a rapid shake, or ∼∼∼∼ , a more relaxed shake). The children will soon discover which kinds of rhythmic patterns are easy to play, or sound best, on which kinds of instruments. It is difficult to play fast complex rhythms on a triangle or Indian bells, and not really very successful on a resonant cymbal, metallophone or glockenspiel; it is much easier on a hand drum or bongos than on a drum hit with one or more sticks. Castanets demand some percussion technique to manage fast rhythms like the typical Spanish ones. But complex rhythms are not too difficult to play on claves, rhythm sticks or wood-block. Scrapers are best used for long scraped and tapped rhythms, while on shakers and maracas complicated rhythms can be managed more easily if the player has a pair of instruments. Of the more sophisticated instruments, the recorder is better for playing a legato (smooth, joined) melody than piano or guitar; other orchestral instruments can be used to play legato melodies, but the technical standard of the player has to be taken into consideration.

In the following list some explanation is given of the less familiar entries in instrument dealers' catalogues. The best way to find out about them, of course, is to go to a well-stocked shop—or better still, a well-stocked school where they can be tried out. Unpitched instruments (or single note instruments like tambours or teacups) have been dealt with first, and then the pitched. One should always buy the best quality instrument possible, for they offer a much wider range of potential sounds. This is especially true of cymbals and glockenspiels. One good glockenspiel is far preferable to ten 'tinny' ones whose notes have no sustaining power at all and whose pitch is scarcely distinguishable. In general one can expect a good quality sound from a manufactured instrument; less resonant sounds can just as easily be produced by home-made instruments constructed from a box of scrap materials that should always be available in the classroom.

METAL INSTRUMENTS
Triangles It is good to have a great variety of sizes available, all made of good quality steel. Rapid rhythms are easier to play near the angles.

Indian bells or Indian cymbals These are two heavy brass cymbals of small diameter which make a high ringing bell-like sound when struck together, the edge of one against the flat surface of the other.

Finger cymbals These are very similar to Indian bells but made of a thinner metal. They can be bought in pitched sets, but these are often expensive.

Sleigh-bells There are a variety of types available with quite different sound qualities. They can be played rhythmically by holding them in one hand and tapping the wooden handle with the other.

Cymbals These have perhaps the greatest range of sounds available of any single instrument. It is worth buying a really good large one, possibly on a stand. The better ones are made of spun steel (the rings from the machine-turning can be seen). Cheaper ones have a poor tinny sound, and can really only be used in pairs struck together, when two saucepan lids would do just as well. All the beaters mentioned below can be used on a single cymbal. The sound quality will also change according to whether it is hit near the edge or the centre, or even on the centre boss, and a very unusual sound can be produced by rubbing a cello or violin bow across the edge as shown below:

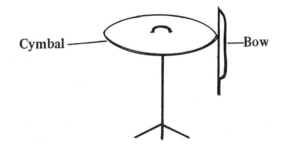

Gongs The orchestral gong or tam-tam has great sound-making potential but is very expensive and hard to come by, although some households—and some antique shops—still have the solid brass dinner-gongs that were so fashionable at the end of the last century. The better the gong, the bigger the range of sounds available. Old brake drums will also make quite good gongs; a metal beater or wooden hammer are best for hitting these.

Bells A variety of bells, besides the more sophisticated sets of tubular bells, make fleeting appearances in orchestral scores. Cow-bells can be struck with triangle beaters and an ordinary school bell (or fire bell) will play more rhythmically if the internal tongue is held still and the bell struck with a different beater.

SKIN-COVERED INSTRUMENTS
Tambours It is desirable to have drums of various sizes. The ones that can be tuned (which have a head held by a ring with tuning pegs) often have a bigger sound range. It is worth experimenting with a variety of beaters on these.

Bass drum or Tenor drum Try to have either a very large tambour or one of these really large drums to produce a good deep sound.

Side drum or Snare drum   This differs from the previous drums in that it is a double-sided drum with wires stretched tightly across one of its skins. This gives it its distinctive sharp quality. A good orchestral side drum on a stand can produce a wide range of sounds, but this demands a fair degree of technical skill. (It is often thought to be the most difficult of the orchestral percussion to play.) The poor imitation of the instrument that often appeared in percussion bands produces a rather weak sound; the tambour sounds are much better. One can produce a sound more like the orchestral instrument by stretching strings of shells, beans or beads over a drum skin lashed to a wooden bowl or box. For more detailed instructions on how to make this, see Ronald Roberts' *Instruments made to be played* (listed in the bibliography at the end of this chapter).

Bongos   These are smaller drums made in pairs. The two drums, which are joined together, are of slightly different sizes and therefore different pitches. They are played with flat hands and can cope with quite complicated rhythms.

Hand drums   These are similar to bongos but are single drums played with the hand or fingers. They are sold in sets of various sizes.

Home-made drums   Single-headed drums can be made by cutting out one end of a tin at least twelve cm long and ten cm in diameter and stretching a piece of vellum (obtainable from music shops) or rubber inner-tube across the open end. A double-headed drum can be made from small or large cans with two heads of rubber inner-tube or vellum lashed together with cord around the side of the tin, in a zigzag pattern, holding them in place. The bigger the tin, the thicker the skin required. Thin strong string is needed and the holes in the skin should not be too close together (about one inch apart) or too near the edge, or they will pull out. Test the note it makes before tying the lashing; if the note is not clear, tighten the skin gently. More detailed instructions can be found in Ronald Roberts' *Instruments made to be played*.

WOODEN INSTRUMENTS

Wood-block   This is a solid wooden block made of hard wood, often rosewood, with a slit cut in it. It is hit with a small wooden beater. Some have a slit on each side, one higher than the other, which gives two different pitches.

Wood-box   This differs from the above only in that it is hollow, which gives it a quite different sound. It usually consists of a wooden tube on the end of a central handle, with slits of differing lengths in each side, thus giving it two notes:

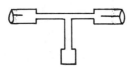

Claves   These are two hardwood (usually ebony) sticks hit together. Pale imitations of them are called rhythm sticks; these are usually much cheaper, and can be hand made from dowelling. Try to have one pair of good manufactured ones: their tone has more penetration and bite.

Castanets Those on a handle and consisting of two—or better still, one—wooden flaps fitting a central wooden piece are much easier to operate than the Spanish finger kind. These require great finger skill if more than well-spaced single taps are to be achieved. A pair mounted on a wood block with springs, such as those used in an orchestra, are even easier to manage but more expensive to buy.

Scraper; Guiro or Reso-Reso Scraper This is basically a wide-diameter piece of bamboo, or a gourd, with notches cut in its side. A wooden or bone stick is rubbed over these notches giving a distinctive sound quite unlike that of any other instrument. The pitch varies according to how close together the notches are; sometimes there are two sets of notches on one instrument. The tone varies depending on how quickly you scrape. If some bamboo is available this can be home-made. Those made from gourds look like space rockets!

Whip In the orchestra this consists of two pieces of wood joined by a hinge and brought smartly together to give a sound like the crack of a whip. Two long lino strips will do just as well.

Coconut Shells These are perhaps the oldest sound effect in use. Two half-shells struck together make a sound like the wood-box.

SHAKEN INSTRUMENTS *(or instruments that sound like them)*
Tambourine This is, as one might guess, related to the tambour, but it has metal jingles let into the side. There is an astonishing difference in quality between various instruments: avoid the horrible tin toy ones. It is not a catastrophe when the vellum head breaks, as the remaining ring of jingles can be struck rhythmically against the hand. This instrument has the added attraction of being a favourite among folk groups.

Maracas These are gourds filled with seeds, ideally played in pairs. A good pair made from real gourds produces an excellent sound but will not withstand a great deal of rough treatment. Once cracked, their sound is poor.

Shakers These are probably the most successful of home-made instruments. Proper maracas can be made by gluing strips of paper (papier mâché) round a plasticine form, cutting it in half, then removing the plasticine and filling it with seeds, and sticking the two halves together again with a handle between them:

A strong glue will give a better quality sound. As an alternative, a light bulb can be used as a form and smashed afterwards to provide the filling. The range of materials suitable for making shakers is vast. The containers can be made of wood (such as bamboo), plastic, cardboard or metal, and the fillings from seeds, ball-bearings, shot, rice, sugar, gravel, sand, stones, broken glass, pins and so forth. Always make sure that the lids are firmly sealed. Once made, these instruments give great scope for artistic decoration.

Lagerphone This is a broom-handle with bottle-tops nailed loosely along it so that they can be shaken. The bottle-tops must have all cork removed and the hole should be drilled centrally. They make an even better sound if nailed in pairs. A rubber door-stopper fastened to the end of the broomstick enables it to be banged rhythmically on the floor.

Milk Rustle This is like the lagerphone, but the noise is produced by strings of milk-bottle tops fastened to the top of the broom-handle and hanging free, which gives it a much gentler sound.

Sandpaper Blocks These are blocks of wood, with sandpaper stuck to them, that are rubbed together. If there is no wood available, ordinary sandpaper sheets will do, but these are harder to control.

Rustles Various types of paper produce rustling sounds: tissue, cellophane, greaseproof and so on. Dry leaves will also produce good rustles. This can be done rhythmically.

Stones and Shells These can be struck together rhythmically, different sizes producing different pitches.

A Wobble-board This is a sheet of thin wood (such as plywood) which when shaken produces a very distinctive sound. It is a relation of the thunder sheet, the thin sheet of metal used to create thunder effects in theatrical productions.

Wind-chimes This instrument is like the wind-chimes found in the Far East and consists of thin sheets of metal hanging on the end of strings which are attached to a wooden bar. When shaken it produces an attractive tinkling sound.

BEATERS
Padded felt These can be improvised out of old cotton-headed washing-up mops.

Wooden There are the round-headed type used for glockenspiels and wood-block, and the straight drumstick type, which can be made out of dowelling.

Metal These are supplied with triangles but can be used to good effect on xylophone or glockenspiel. They are essential for hitting flowerpots, teacups and glasses (see p. 37-8).

Rubber These are sold for use with chime bars but produce interesting sounds on other instruments.

Wire brushes These are part of a sidedrummer's equipment and are well worth investing in for interesting drum and cymbal effects.

Bundle of twigs This produces the same effect as coarse wire brushes, and can also be used as rustles.

Sandpaper Used gently on the surface of a drum it produces an effect similar to that of the wire brushes.

Cello or violin bow   This produces interesting effects on a cymbal (see p. 33).

Hands   These can be used flat, and the fingers can manage soft but complicated rhythms.

PITCHED INSTRUMENTS
Glockenspiels   These have steel keys and good ones produce a fine resonant sound. Cheap ones may sound very tinny.

Xylophones   These have wooden keys mounted on a resonating box. Home-made xylophones can be made from strips of wood of various lengths strung together, but they often lack the resonance of manufactured ones. A bass xylophone, if it can be afforded, is an extremely useful instrument with a splendid sound.

Metallophone   This is a most beautiful instrument and is a great favourite with children. It has the resonating box of the xylophone with large, thick steel keys. It makes a gentle bell-like sound, and its glissando is particularly beautiful.

[*Note:* The glissando effect can be obtained on all three of the instruments mentioned above by running a beater over the keys. All these instruments are made in several sizes and ideally it is desirable to own a good selection. It is better to buy the type with removable keys or bars, as these can be used more easily for tunes of limited range (see p. 24) or pentatonic compositions (see pp. 24-25) by removing the unnecessary bars. It is not vital to own chromatic versions of these instruments, these have all the sharps and flats as well as the white notes of the piano keyboard. Most diatonic instruments are supplied with B♭ and F♯ which makes it possible to use the scales of G major and F major as well as C major. If a chromatic instrument can be afforded, look for the type in which the black notes are mounted on a separate box; this can also be used as a separate pentatonic scale (see p. 24).]

Chime Bars   These are steel plates mounted on wooden tube resonators. They are available in pitched sets sold either mounted in a box (from which they can be removed, but which is very useful for storage) or separately. They make a bell-like sound when hit with the beater supplied with them, but can also be hit with other beaters; a vibrato effect can be achieved by hitting them and passing a strip of cardboard back and forth over the hole in the wooden tube. Chime bars have the advantage of being suitable for splitting up and distributing between the children. This is particularly useful for pieces requiring a chordal accompaniment (see pp. 25 et seq.).

Bottles   A collection of bottles of various sizes is very useful. They will produce different notes when empty, but can be more carefully tuned by filling them with small amounts of water. The best sound is produced by blowing across the top with the bottle resting in the curve of the lower lip and the upper lip half over the hole. To produce a well-defined note, make a 't' sound like spitting out a pip, similar to the one used in tonguing notes on the recorder. (The same technique is used for blowing across a pen top.) They can also be struck with a metal beater.

Glasses   These can be tuned like the bottles and can also be struck. If the glasses are thin enough, they can also be set in vibration by rubbing a moistened finger round the rim. (This is related to the work of *Les Structures Sonores* (LD066M), a group of French musicians who make music on long glass rods. Their records are obtainable from Discurio, 9 Shepherd Street, London W1, on the Avion label.)

Teacups Benjamin Britten uses a scale of teacups in *Noye's Fludde* to represent raindrops. Children can have great fun in choosing teacups tuned to one another. These can be suspended from a wooden bar and struck with a metal beater.

Flowerpots Earthenware ones are not easy to find, but are worth keeping, for they can be used for a variety of effects. They can be suspended upside down like the teacups, with string through their holes, and then struck with a metal beater; different sizes will produce different notes. Up the right way, they can either be 'stirred' with a metal beater or struck with a more rapid movement of the beater from side to side. The sounds they produce are quite distinctive.

OTHER PITCHED INSTRUMENTS
(These are the most commonly found, but of course one should make use of any expertise that one finds in a class.)

Piano This is an overworked instrument, and inconvenient in that its player normally has at least half his back to the class. It is not an ideal melodic instrument because it does not produce a good legato sound, especially at the hands of inexperienced players. But a curious legato effect can be created on tape by taking a melody played on a piano and carefully editing out (cutting off) the tape between each note to produce one continuous sound with the notes running one into the other. The piano can, however, be very useful for playing low ostinato patterns, as it is often the only bass instrument that a school possesses (see p. 18). If the strings of the piano can be exposed—which is easy to do on a grand piano but not so easy on an upright, when the front needs to be removed—some interesting effects can be obtained by running the fingers over them. The effect produced is not unlike the sound of the harp. A poem like Enitharmon's song (from *The Four Zoas, Night the Second*) by Blake provides great scope for using this effect, and could be accompanied by unpitched effects as well:

> I seize the sphery harp, I strike the strings.
> At the first sound the golden sun arises from the deep
> And shakes his awful hair,
> The echo wakes the moon to unbind her silver locks,
> The golden sun bears on my song
> And nine bright spheres of harmony rise round the fiery king. . . .

Another technique used by contemporary composers is that of playing note clusters. This involves laying either the flat of the hand, or the hand and forearm, on the keyboard so that a number of adjacent notes are played simultaneously. Interesting effects can be made with these clusters, especially if there is more than one player at the keyboard at a time (see p. 63). One must guard against playing too many clusters simultaneously; the two players should concentrate on varying the pitch and the rhythmic patterns.

Contemporary composers are also using what are called 'prepared pianos'. The 'preparation' is done by sticking small buttons, coins, pieces of silver foil and wire between the strings before playing in the usual way; this produces a very unusual sound.

Guitar   This is a more suitable instrument for accompaniment, because the player sits facing the class. It is also unlikely to drown the singing; indeed, the problem is often that of producing sufficient volume, especially from a Spanish-style guitar with nylon strings. The 'scratch' technique is often the best to use on these instruments and probably the simplest too. (A good guitar tutor is John Pearse's *Teach Yourself Folk Guitar* published by Saga.) The guitar will be much easier to use if the teacher has a sure singing voice with which to lead, because playing a melody will be more difficult than on the piano. One of the recorder players might be a great help here. However, when the song has been learned, a guitar is invaluable for helping the class to hold a tune without other assistance. The easier keys to play are E and A minor and G and D major.

The guitar can be used in creative work for playing ostinati, and children who have not learned to play the instrument properly can still manage simple open-string patterns, although these will have to be fairly slow and uncomplicated:

Interesting rhythms can also be created by drumming the fingers on the wood of the instrument.

Recorders   These are very useful melodic instruments, particularly if there are some skilful players in the class. Once more, an assortment of instruments of different sizes is invaluable. It is possible to play melodic improvisations on them (see p. 22), and a variety of effects is obtainable, from trills (quick alternation of adjacent notes) and tremolos (quick alternation of notes further apart) to a variety of whistle sounds made by using the mouthpiece alone, without the lower joints.

Bamboo Pipes   These produce a more mellow and gentler sound than recorders. They can be made by the children themselves, gradually boring more holes as they learn to play more and more notes. Tuning them provides good practice in aural perception. Detailed instructions for constructing them can be found in M. Galloway's book *Making and Playing Bamboo Pipes* (Dryad Press).

Melodica   This is a relation of the accordion in that it has both piano keyboard and reeds, but the air is blown in through a mouthpiece. It can play melodies and chords and comes in various sizes. Its tone, however, is very strident and will overbalance almost all the instruments mentioned so far. Its most valuable use is therefore for accompanying or reinforcing a tune sung by a large group of people.

Kazoo   This is a sophisticated 'comb and paper': a round hollow metal or plastic rocket-shaped barrel with a grill let into it, over which is stretched tissue paper. The pitch is changed by the player humming into it. It is a favourite instrument amongst folk singers and is very useful if pupils are too self-conscious to improvise vocally (see p. 22). It also has the advantage of being inexpensive.

STRINGED INSTRUMENTS

If these are used in creative work the class teacher should be very careful not to undermine the technique that the instrumental teacher is trying to build up. Improvising requires a certain degree of technical skill in order for the pupil to concentrate on the improvisation alone rather than on technical difficulties. Interesting effects can be obtained by using glissando (sliding the fingers of the left hand up and down the string), pizzicato (plucking) or using the wood of the bow. Harmonics (made by resting the finger lightly on the string at specific points) give an unusual, mysterious sound if the player knows how and where to produce them.

This is by no means an exhaustive list of instruments but simply some that will prove useful. If others are available, experiment with them to find out their sound potential and see how they can most satisfactorily be used.

BIBLIOGRAPHY

Blocksidge, K. M.: *Making musical apparatus and instruments,* University of London Press.

Jeans, Sir James: *Science and Music,* Cambridge University Press.

Mandell and Wood: *Make your own musical instruments,* Sterling Publishing Co., New York.

Roberts, Ronald: *Instruments made to be played,* Dryad Press.

Part Two
THE PROJECTS

Each project is laid out in three sections. The A section suggests how one might start the project with the class as a whole. For this activity sit the children in a circle, each with an instrument (see p. 10). It is probably better at first to allocate the instruments arbitrarily and only allow the children to choose for themselves later in the project. The B section suggests how the children's individual contributions can be linked together and developed into a class composition. This is still, of course, an activity for the class as a whole. The C section contains a list of the variety of ways in which the project can then be developed further. Some are ideas for group work forming a suite of pieces around the theme of the project; others are completely new ideas for class activities. Some suggest listening material, while others suggest related art, drama and dance projects; in some cases these can be linked together to form a presentation using several media.

Remember that all the musical ideas in the projects are only suggestions and the way in which you develop each one depends to a large extent on the ideas the children put forward. The projects should be used only if ideas run out, when it is very useful to have something 'up your sleeve'. Use them only in these cases, and do not impose them too heavily at the start. There is a very fine balance between giving sufficient stimulus to get a project started and giving so much guidance that the children cannot use their own ideas at all. It is really better after the initial introduction to feed ideas in gradually. As children get used to this type of work you will find that they need less and less help.

The projects are not arranged in order of difficulty. The last three projects, which involve stories, will probably take longer, and are more complex in that they involve the creation of a variety of pieces and probably some group work. Group work should only be attempted when the class has had some experience of working as a class unit. Light (Project 1) or Fire (Project 5, p. 59) are good ones to start with.

Project 1
LIGHT

A   Begin by asking each child to create a sound that is suggested to him by the word 'light'. This provokes a variety of responses and will lead to a discussion about the various kinds of light.

B   The poem 'Sunbright, daylight' by Cecily Taylor provides a useful co-ordinator of some of the sounds suggested and may extend the children's imagination. The poem may be spoken with the sounds as a background, or spaces may be left for them. As the latter method upsets the rhythm of the poem, it is better to say it slowly, perhaps in choral speech for the sake of balance between voice and music (see pp. 29-30). The following are only suggestions for musical treatment and some verses have been left without suggestions. Ideally one should use the sounds the children produce in the first activity, developing them to illustrate the poem.

Verse 1   Opening music: impression of darkness, possibly a xylophone glissando with a padded stick,

Sunbright,
cymbal crash

daylight,
glissando on metallophone

Stars in darkest night,
Indian cymbal

Glow-worm,
isolated notes on a
xylophone with a metal stick

candlelight,
triangle

Christmas tree,
taps on a tambourine

and birthday lights:
tambourine shake

Verse 2   See suggestions under section C of Project 5 for firework music.

Sparklers, matchlight,
Rockets—what-a-sight!
Look out—jumping light,
Golden Rain on bonfire night:

Verse 3   Opening music: impression of the 'busy-ness' of the city (see p. 14).

Shop lights glare white,
Posters neon-bright,
Headlights, traffic lights,
Ambulance with flashing light:

Verse 4 Opening music: impression of excitement and happiness.

Floodlight, spotlight,
Usherette's torchlight,
Swing-boat hold-on-tight,
Roundabout and fairground lights:

Verse 5 Opening music: ?

Ship lights flare white,
Lighthouse guiding bright,
Train lights, station lights,
Signal box and warning lights:

Verse 6 Opening music: ?

Moonlight,
wire brushes on a large cymbal

spaceflight,
*shake with a crescendo from a
shaker filled with dried peas*

Beacon
*tremolo on two notes near
middle of a metallophone*

satellite,
*shake with a crescendo from
a shaker filled with seeds*

Red light from a height—
*tremolo on two notes high on
a glockenspiel*

Aeroplane and runway lights:
drum roll with a crescendo

Verse 7 Opening music: this might include a swaying pattern on the metallophone
to suggest the rocking movement of a lullaby:

This could be continued throughout the verse.

Coach light,
find an interesting chord of
three notes high on a
metallophone, e.g:

lamplight,
find an interesting chord of
three notes low on a metallophone, e.g:

Porch light,
on chime bars

home-in-sight,
on chime bars

Bath light,
on a high glockenspiel

bedside light,
on a lower glockenspiel

Put-it-out and say goodnight!
claves leading to opening
'darkness' music.

Further suggestions for musical treatment of the poem as a song can be found in the book *New Horizons,* published by Galliard, 1974.

C   1   Use the beginning of the story of the Creation from Genesis as a stimulus. One could start in many ways; here are two suggestions:

(a) Set the children to work in pairs before telling them which story they are working on. The instruments in each pair should be contrasted (for example, a metal instrument like a triangle with a wooden one like a scraper). One child should choose darkness and the other light, after deciding which instrument is suitable for each. Ask them to arrange a musical contest between the two, showing clearly which one wins. The character and atmosphere of the light and the darkness should be established either by rhythm or tone colour before the contest. Does one power overcome the other gradually, or does it conquer with a sudden stroke? What is the most satisfactory way of portraying victory musically? Having done this preparatory work, some of the ideas may be used in the story.

(b) Use words to portray the darkness and light. Words can be used for their colour or for their meaning. In the suggestions that follow, you will notice that the groups are using words for their colour: long 'oo' words for chaos, long 'aa' words for darkness, long 'o' words for emptiness and 'ee' words for depth. But one might also use words for their meaning: group 1 could use 'chaos', 'disorder', 'confusion'; group 2, 'void', 'nothing', 'emptiness'; group 3, 'darkness', 'blackness', 'night'; and group 4, 'abyss', 'depth', 'profound'. Ideally, the children should choose their own words once they have understood the principle (see p. 15).

THE BEGINNING OF CREATION

NARRATOR	MUSIC

Use a few words suggesting chaos to be said
in canon very softly:
e.g.

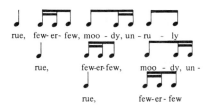

Group 1: Continue the 'oo' sounds.

In the beginning of creation, when God
made heaven and earth, the earth was
without form

Group 2: Use words suggesting emptiness.

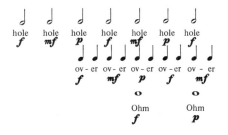

and void,

Continue the sounds very softly.

with darkness

Group 3: Use words to suggest darkness.

Continue the sounds very softly.

over the face of the abyss,

Group 4: Use words suggesting depth.

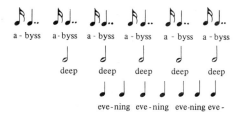

Continue the sounds very softly.

and the spirit swept over the surface of the waters.

What sort of spirit? Is it a rushing wind or a gentle movement? Is it the beginning of the light music? Should it have any connection with the light music? Would a glissando on a glockenspiel be suitable? (A practical point: can it be heard above the sounds already being played?)

If the alternative translation in the NEB is taken—'a mighty wind' rather than 'the spirit'—any idle member of the class may be employed in making the sound of the wind. The problems of various translations might be discussed with the class.

God said, 'Let there be light',

How will you represent God speaking? Should everyone say these words? Should they be accompanied by chords on pitched instruments such as chime bars and guitars? Should they be said or sung? Should the music be loud or soft? Should it grow out of the spirit music already created?

and there was light;

This can employ ideas from previous class exercises or from the introductory activity described in C(a), or some new concept may be required. Is it a sudden blaze or a gradual process? Are the sounds of darkness still to continue or should they be completely conquered?

and God saw that the light was good . . .

Continue the sounds of light during these words, making sure it is brought to a satisfactory climax and ending.

The work on this story might be followed by listening to 'The Representation of Chaos' and the first chorus from Haydn's *Creation*.

2 Take part of the first verse of this poem 'The World' by Henry Vaughan:

Tape recorded drum sounds slowed down, producing a low booming sound, could be used to introduce the poem.

I saw Eternity the other night
Like a great Ring of pure and endless light,

Bright sounds: a slow trill on a triangle, bells, finger cymbals. (If these are tuned, a 'circular' tune could be created, e.g. DED♯ C♯BC♮)

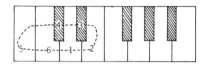

All calm, as it was bright
And round beneath it, Time in hours, days, years

Use a steady tap on the wood block continuing until the word 'hurl'd'.

Driv'n by the spheres
Like a vast shadow mov'd, In which the world
And all her train were hurl'd . . .

Maracas ◁▭▷

A glissando down from the top of the highest glockenspiel to the bottom of the bass xylophone.

3. Discussion after the Henry Vaughan poem might lead to the subjects of heaven and hell, which are often associated with ideas of light and darkness, as this poem 'Death' by 11-year-old Susan Pyke shows. It could well be treated musically: see the notes at the side.

DEATH

SPEECH   MUSIC

This could be introduced by a funeral march with deep drum. If an ostinato pattern is created it could be continued throughout the song.

"Pride-hurting and painful and then;"

Use sharp sounds from the castanet or wood-block, or experiment with a football rattle.

"Dark"

A sudden contrast, perhaps using the dark sounds previously used in the Creation story.

"Just dark and no more thoughts"
"Of suffering and pain."
"Burning fires of Hades,"
"Flickering, jumping, leaping,"
"Twisting and twirling around."

'Fire' music with emphasis on the burning, perhaps using cymbal sounds. It might be related to the sharp sounds of line one, further intensified by the cymbal.

"Death and darkness are coming,"
"But what will be his means of"
"Killing me?"

The 'darkness' music heard in the distance.

?

Perhaps the class could listen to some composers' musical ideas about death. Passages from Elgar's *Dream of Gerontius* or Strauss's *Death and Transfiguration* might be used if the class atmosphere is suitable.

4 Try a space project using sound on tape speeded up or slowed down. For this you really need two tape recorders that can be linked together (see p. 31). This passage of Walt Whitman's, describing the night of 18 March 1879 on the Delaware, might prove a starting point for the project.

SPEECH

MUSIC

One of the calm, pleasantly cool, exquisitely clear and cloudless early spring nights—the atmosphere again that rare vitreous blue-black, welcom'd by astronomers. Just at eight, evening, the scene overhead of certainly solemnest beauty, never surpass'd. Venus nearly down in the west, of a size and lustre as if trying to outshow herself, before departing. . . .

Either the strings of the piano stroked or a roll on a large drum played at a slower speed.

A large cymbal crash either at the correct speed or slowed down.

Arcturus is now risen, just north of east. In calm glory all the stars of Orion hold the place of honour, in meridian, to the south—with the Dog-star a little to the left. And now, just rising, Spica, late, low, and slightly veil'd. Castor, Regulus and the rest, all shining unusually clear, (no Mars or Jupiter or moon till morning). On the edges of the river many lamps twinkling—

Experiment with metal sounds at various speeds, for example: water glasses struck; chime bars used with the vibrato technique described on p. 37; cow bells.

Experiment with showers of small metal sound at fast speeds, for example: rhythms on an Indian cymbal, glockenspiel, or triangle; showering cutlery on to a wooden table; jangling a bunch of keys; plucking the strings of a piano; Japanese wind-chimes (see p. 36).

with two or three huge chimneys, a couple of miles up, belching forth molten, steady flames volcano-like, illuminating all around—and sometimes an electric or calcium, its Dante-Inferno gleams, in far shafts, terrible, ghastly, powerful.

Try slowing down on tape: a tambourine shake; a violin glissando; a cymbal rubbed with a wire brush; a spin-dryer starting up.

Use the passage as an inspiration for sounds and then arrange them by editing the tape into any order you like for a composition called 'The Sky' or 'Space'. The project might be linked with pictures and photographs. You could conclude by listening to any records of electronic music the school has available and asking the children to find out about the use of electronic music in drama on television and radio and the work of the BBC Radiophonic Workshop.

PROJECT 2
DAWN

[*Note:* Projects 2, 3 and 4 can be worked together to form a sequence called 'The Day'.]

A   Discuss night. Do the children find it frightening or friendly? Is it noisier or more silent than day? Get each child to give his impression of night on his instrument. See that some children have paper to rustle besides having wooden and skin instruments like drums and scrapers available. If you have a xylophone the player could be encouraged to create a pattern that can be repeated; for instance:

B   Organise the children's sounds around this ostinato played slowly. The children should be given a place in relation to the ostinato: paper rustle on beat one, the wood-block on beat two, and so on:

It might be interesting for the class to listen to Bartok's 'Night Music' (Universal Edition). It is not an easy piece to listen to, but it does have a strong atmosphere.

C   1   Read through the three poems used in the following project:
'How goes the night?' translated from the Chinese by Helen Waddell (Speakers 1, 2, 3 and 4);
'Cold, clear and blue' by Emily Bronte (Speaker 5);
'Shine out, fair sun', an anonymous sixteenth-century English poem (Speaker 6).

50

Discuss with the children what sort of music would be appropriate. Then set groups to work on:

(a) the flame music Suggestions for these
(b) the throbbing of the drum three are included in
(c) the star music the worked-out project

(d) the fanfare music. Try using three recorders in close-position harmony. Use strong vigorous rhythms with some repeated notes. This is a complex example. It can be simplified by playing as far as (X) only.

(e) the dance of the sun. The music from the class project on the sun might be used here. Whether or not or how much of it is used will depend on whether 'Noon' is being performed. Should the tune be a dancing one like a folk tune on a recorder? Or should it be more like a ceremonial march with the cymbal crash prominent? Alternatively, perhaps there should be an atmosphere of radiance created by high- and low-sounding metal instruments (see pp. 32-3). For example:

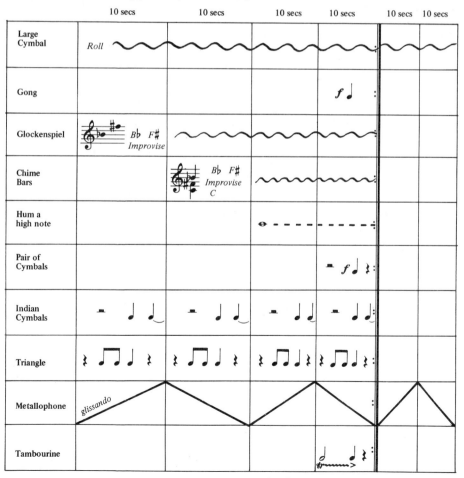

Include any other pieces the class thinks suitable.

2 Look at pictures of different kinds of clouds, and then paint pictures using their shapes. Look at the stars and use their shapes to make patterns.

3 Discuss movements which might help to illustrate the poems. Everyone should try the movements to start with, although five special groups of dancers might be used for the final product. Label their roles by giving them strips of differently coloured material to wear:

    Group A—darkness: black

    Group B—fire: orange

    Group C—dawn clouds: pale blue

    Group D—the star: pale grey

    Group E—the sun: golden.

4 Now fit the whole project together. The following details are only suggestions; your own project will obviously follow the lines indicated by your pupils. The layout suggests how the three aspects of the project—speech divided between different speakers, musicians, and dancers—happen simultaneously. The musicians may be grouped on either side of the stage, one group representing darkness and the others light. The poems are intertwined with one another and the use of different speakers gives opportunities for stereophonic effects, which can be achieved by placing readers apart from one another.

DAWN

SPEECH	MUSIC	MOVEMENT
[*Poem*: 'How Goes the Night']		
Speaker 1 How goes the night?	Use the 'night' music, perhaps scaled down from the full class composition so that it can be played by a smaller number of children.	Base the opening on the picture of clouds already looked at. At each sound in the music, a new dancer might appear.
Speaker 2 Midnight has still to come.		Gradually the black dancers (Group A) move in low swirly movements until they come to rest in a tightly knit semi-circle at the back of the stage.
Speaker 3 Down in the court the torch is blazing bright,	Flame music: Tongues of flame represented by shakes of the tambourine or rapid glissandi up and down a glockenspiel. (This could be a part of the larger project on fire.)	A few dancers with bright orange scarves (Group B) perform leaping movements.
Speaker 4 Hear far off the throbbing of the drum.	Throbbing of the drum: A very bold rhythm is needed preferably simply with crotchets and quavers. It is probably better played on a drum with two wooden sticks, although two padded sticks on a tambour would also be possible. Ideally the player improvises, but a repetitive pattern of this kind would do:	As the drum beats, the black dancers (Group A) swirl around the stage again.
	It gets louder.	

SPEECH	MUSIC	MOVEMENT
Speaker 5 Cold, clear, and blue, the morning heaven Extends its arch on high;	The star music: over the drum rhythm, the pattern chosen for the morning star appears. Groups of three notes on a glockenspiel (*cold, clear, blue*) are a possible choice.	The blue-scarved dancers (Group C) come from the side, surround the black ones, and gradually force them lower and lower until they finally lie on the ground. The movement of the dancers could be synchronised with the glockenspiel clusters, pressing up over the dark dancers; or it might be a smoother movement for which glissandi could be played on a second glockenspiel, the dancers moving to a formation of arches.
Cold, clear, and blue, Lake Werna's water Reflects that winter's sky.	Keep this pattern going above the glissandi low down on the metallophone.	A few dancers (Group D) make low slow swirling movements and form a pattern the same as Group C, but kneeling.
The moon has set, but Venus shines A silent, silvery star.	Chime bars in a cluster played together, e.g. Create patterns with bright metallic instruments—triangle, Indian cymbal, bells. Repeat the chime bar chord in the background.	One solo dancer in a grey scarf represents the star. Use the same shapes you have made in your star painting.
Speaker 1 How goes the night?	A short reprise of some of the night music. Keep the xylophone ostinato going through the whole of the next section.	Group A rises slightly and moves round the blue dancers with the star.
Speaker 2 The night is not yet gone.		
Speaker 3 I hear the trumpets blazing on the heights.	The fanfare music (see p. 51).	The three groups of dancers (A, C and D) gradually intermingle, making various shapes.

	SPEECH	MUSIC	MOVEMENT
Speaker 4	The torch is paling in the coming dawn.	Reprise of flame music.	The torch dancers (Group B) come on, leap about and 'die'.
Speaker 6	Shine out, fair sun, with all your heat, Show all your thousand-colour'd light! Black Winter freezes to his seat; The grey wolf howls, he does so bite; Crookt Age on three knees creeps the street; The boneless fish close quaking lies And eats for cold his aching feet; The stars in icicles arise: Shine out, and make this winter night Our beauty's Spring, our Prince of Light.	Keep the xylophone ostinato going. Downward glissandi on other xylophones. A really good original sound is needed here; perhaps some of the metallic pitched instruments should be saved for this moment. A large gong or cymbal may be suitable. After the initial crash a roll may be kept going to lead into the Dance of the Sun.	The three groups of dancers (ACD) close into a circle, leaning to the centre, black dancers outermost and the star in the middle. Gradually the black dancers unwind from the circle. The star moves away. A single dancer (with golden scarf) leaps into the middle of the blue dancers. She is followed by other golden dancers (Group E) who pair off with the blue dancers in a gay dance.
Speaker 1	How goes the night?		Is the radiance of the sun peaceful or vigorous? What sort of pattern does sunlight make? Use the contrast between blue and gold dancers to create either sunlight or cloud patterns.
Speaker 2	The night is past and done.		
Speaker 3	The torch is smoking in the morning light.		
Speaker 4	The dragon banner floating in the sun.		

Project 3
NOON

A Let the class find out all they can about the sun. Look not only at the modern astronomical and scientific aspects but also at primitive man's worship of the sun and his fear of the eclipse. Let each child choose an instrument to represent his findings.

B One might then combine the various pictures into a rondo form, so that every child's offering is used. The best one can be used as the main theme of the rondo (A). Then the other groups' compositions can form the intervening sections in an ABACADA pattern (see pp. 16-17). Movement for this can be created to suit the music.

C This passage by Jeremy Taylor could provide a good starting point for a piece exploring the various sounds which can be made on a large cymbal (or perhaps a selection of cymbals of various sizes).

But as when the Sun approaches towards the gates	Use a violin bow on the edge of the cymbal (see p. 33).
of the morning, he first opens a little eye of Heaven,	Use a wire brush on the very edge of the cymbal.
and sends away the spirits of darkness,	Gentle roll on cymbal with padded stick near the edge.
and gives light to a cock,	An Indian cymbal or perhaps a rubber beater near the centre of a large cymbal.
and calls up the lark to Mattins,	Strokes on the cymbal with wooden stick.
and by and by gilds the fringes of a cloud,	A variety of small cymbals or a roll with wire brushes.
and peeps over the eastern hills,	A metal beater on the centre boss.
thrusting out his golden horns, like those which decked the	A roll using a padded stick moving to the centre of the cymbal with a crescendo.
brows of Moses when he was forced to wear a veil, because	
himself had seen the face of God;	
and still while a man tells the story, the sun gets up higher,	
till he shows a fair face and a full light,	All cymbals together, or one strong stroke on the large cymbal.
and then he shines one whole day,	Keep a steady roll going with padded sticks, moderately loud . . .
under a cloud often, and sometimes	getting softer . . .
weeping great and little showers,	rise to a crescendo and then . . .
and sets quickly:	diminuendo . . .
So is a man's reason and his life.	to nothing.

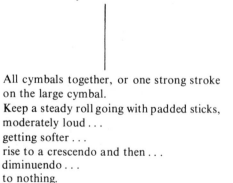

This experimenting can then perhaps be used to make a piece entitled 'The Sun' built around cymbal sounds. This might be easier if put on tape.

Project 4
EVENING

A Create a picture of a peaceful country scene. Ask each child to give his musical impression of one aspect of it. The head joints of recorders or whistles can be used alone to imitate birdsong. Compose a gentle recorder tune (or use a gentle song tune in $\frac{6}{8}$ time) and arrange the sounds around it.

B When you have created satisfactory music for the pastoral scene, set sounds from the Sun Project against it. Then practise, gradually substituting the night sounds from the opening of the Dawn Project in place of the Sun music. Substitute these one or two at a time, with the pastoral tune and sounds continuing, until the accompaniment consists only of dark sounds.

C Create some movement for your music and fit the whole project together. The following is a suggestion based on the poem 'Day's End' by W. H. Bartlett. The movement groups refer to those used in the Dawn Project.

EVENING

SPEECH	MUSIC	MOVEMENT
Speaker The wind cries and the shadow Broods upon the meadow.	Use your countryside music, combined with the sunshine music. Continue this quietly. A glissando up and down the glockenspiel can be used for the wind, or a blowing noise made by the mouth (do not continue this sound). The xylophone glissando is added to the sounds.	As this is played the dancers of Group E move in a circle formation. The dancers of Group A form a wider circle around that of Group E, as far away from them as possible.
Leisurely, through shrinking skies, A single, speckled pigeon flies On comfortable wing To the green glooms welcoming. Oh, hear the waves of night Encroach upon the light And break, in empty curves of sound, On drooping tree and quiet mound, On farm and inoffensive beast Dreaming of tomorrow's feast. The wind sighs and the shadow Bites into the meadow.	One could introduce a new sound in the music here, but the atmosphere must not be broken by it. Discuss this. The ostinato of the darkness music appears (see the Dawn Project). Gradually add some of the sounds of the darkness music one by one. The wind sound should begin here. A repeated tapping from the claves intensifies the darkness sounds.	The outer circle moves in and out in waves, sometimes touching the inner one. There should be increasing contact between the two groups of dancers. The circles break and the dancers intermingle.
With curious call the owls ride The hidden crest of eventide; Beast and building, tree and mound, In an ebon sea are drowned; And through the dew-wet grass and deep Man goes home to his long sleep. The wind dies, and the shadow Swallows up the meadow.	The sun sounds start to drop out one by one. More darkness sounds are added. Descending glissando on the glockenspiel. The scraper part is intensified and the darkness sounds gradually take over.	The black dancers dance high, the gold ones low. The gold dancers scatter and the black take their opening semi-circle to the back.

Project 5
FIRE

A   Describe a fire for the children (many of them may have experienced it only through the television screen). Ask them to shut their eyes and imagine the curling smoke, the glowing ashes, the smouldering, hissing heart of the fire, the jumping sparks, the leaping flames. Then ask each child to choose one aspect of fire and describe it on his instrument.

B   Build up a musical description of a fire by grouping together the ideas of those children who have chosen to describe the same aspect. The listing below contains suggestions to be used in the absence of ideas from the children. To start with, each group comes in together and carries on playing softly as the new sounds enter, so that the piece rises to a gradual climax:

Smoke	Shakers, maracas, humming.
Smouldering, glowing ashes in the heart of the fire	Glissandi up and down a metallophone or xylophone, with isolated notes on chime bars, glockenspiel, triangle or Indian cymbal.
Hiss	vocal 'ss', sandpaper blocks rubbed together, wire brushes on cymbals.
Sparks	lively rhythms on woodblocks, castanets and claves.
Flames	tambourine shakes, side drum rolls, cymbal rolls, a melodic pattern which rises and falls rapidly played on the metallophone and glockenspiel. The span of the notes might grow gradually like this:

This could be linked to a whole movement sequence, or built up bit by bit by exploring each aspect in dance as well as sound.

C   1   Listen to the fire music from Britten's ballet *The Prince of the Pagodas*.

2   Fireworks. One might describe the various types with different tune shapes (see p. 28). Here are some suggestions:

59

Rockets

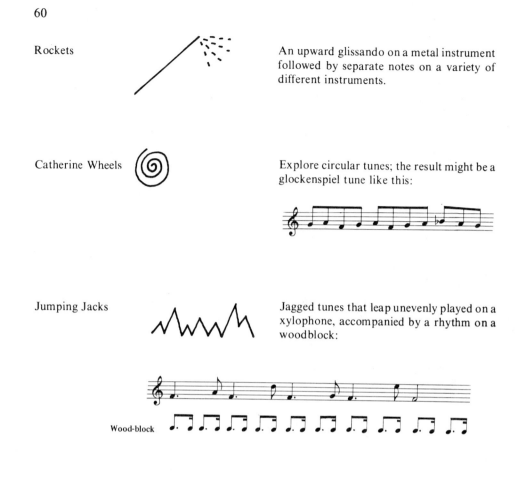

An upward glissando on a metal instrument followed by separate notes on a variety of different instruments.

Catherine Wheels

Explore circular tunes; the result might be a glockenspiel tune like this:

Jumping Jacks

Jagged tunes that leap unevenly played on a xylophone, accompanied by a rhythm on a woodblock:

Wood-block

Roman Candles

Tambourine shake followed by a 'shower' of notes descending on a glockenspiel, or several glockenspiels accompanied by a vocal hiss.

These could be linked with the fire music to give a musical picture of Guy Fawkes Night. Or they could be linked by a rhyme like 'Remember, remember the fifth of November' chanted, spoken or sung between them. This could also be linked with art work.

Listen to Debussy's *Feux d'artifice* ('Fireworks').

3 Heat. Explore clusters of notes played close together on all the instruments available; especially those that can sustain the sound, like recorders, bottles blown across the top, melodicas and humming. Chime bars and metallophone are also possible. Experiment with recording these sounds and making them smoother by editing out the beginning of each note so that they make one long sound.

Make a composition about a piece of coal:

How it started as a tree	Wooden sounds: scraper, maracas, castanets, claves.
How it grew in the sun and trapped its energy	Cymbals and/or metallophone merging softly with the heat music.
How it lay in the swamps for millions of years	Continue heat music softly with a bubbling sound above it (straws in bottles?).
How it releases its energy when it burns	Heat music rises to a crescendo, perhaps leading into some elements of the fire music.

Listen to 'Paludisme' from *Les Structures Sonores* (see p. 38), which is an attempt to portray tropical fever.

Project 6
WEATHER

A Describe a storm to the class. Ask them to imagine a hot day in summer with the sun glistening through the leaves onto the flowers; the white clouds are speeding across the sky but are gradually becoming greyer; in the distance is a faint clap of thunder; the wind rises gradually and starts to howl; the first raindrops start to fall gently, then faster and faster until there is a roaring torrent; gradually the rain slackens, the thunder retreats into the distance and a rainbow glistens in the sky. Let each child choose one aspect of the storm and describe it musically.

B Compose a class storm picture in music: a piece built around the dynamic pattern

$$\overleftarrow{}\quad\overrightarrow{}$$

First, use the sounds of the sunny summer's day. — A recorder tune, perhaps with some gentle sounds from triangle or Indian cymbals.

Above these, introduce the sounds for the clouds which gradually become more intense. — Clusters of notes on a glockenspiel;

Soft sounds of distant thunder (The players could stand at a distance from the class). — roll on a deep drum.

Introduce the sound of the wind. — Vocal sound or shakers;

Add a few isolated raindrop sounds. — isolated notes on chime bars and on teacups or clay flowerpots struck with metal beaters.

As you intensify the thunder, wind and rain, drop the sunny sounds. — Tambourine shakes.

Play louder and louder to a climax, then fade.

Gradually stop the sounds, reintroducing the sunny sounds one by one.

When the sunny sounds have all returned, introduce the sound of the rainbow. — Glissando up and down on a metallophone.

Listen to 'In the Fields' from Berlioz's *Symphonie Fantastique* or the storm from Britten's *Noye's Fludde.*

C Create a suite of pieces about various types of weather. This could be linked with a project on meteorology. One might start the project by asking each child to describe a particular type of weather and then working from a basis of the ideas put forward.

1 Frost and Snow. Take the pattern of the frost as the starting point. Discuss the relationship between geometric and musical shapes. The jagged line of icicles might be suggested by a 'jagged' tune:

or by using a more simple rhythmic pattern:

Here, both the rhythm and the melody is designed to give a jagged effect. If one drew a line joining the heads of the notes (see p. 28), the pattern 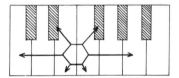 would be obtained, which clearly relates the tune to its visual stimulus of icicles.

The study of frost might lead to a study of crystal patterns; interesting work could then be done transferring these more complex shapes into musical terms. If you were to draw a simplified crystal pattern on a piano keyboard it might turn out something like this:

When played it might sound E♭CE♮FAF♯ which could be put into a rhythmic pattern and used as the basis for a 'Piece in the form of an ice crystal'. It can be varied by playing it high, low, on various instruments, in a variety of rhythms, with a variety of accompaniments, and so forth. Contrast may be achieved by drawing other crystal patterns on a keyboard and working out new tunes. One might also use the same method with the patterns drawn by frost on the window-panes.

Ice crystal shapes could also be put into dance rhythms to make a 'Dance of the Snowflakes'. Listen to Debussy's 'The Snow is Dancing' from the *Children's Corner Suite*.

2 Mist. Use this extract from 'November' by John Clare as a starting point for the exploration of unusual clusters of notes.

> The landscape sleeps in mist from morn till noon;
> And, if the sun looks through, 'tis with a face
> Beamless and pale and round, as if the moon,

When done the journey of her nightly race,
Had found him sleeping, and supplied his place.
For days the shepherds in the fields may be,
Nor mark a patch of sky—blindfold they trace
The plains, that seem without a bush or tree,
Whistling aloud by guess to flocks they cannot see.

Experiment with unusual groups of chime bars, e.g. CEG♯, C♯DE♭, FAC♯, F♯AB♭, GBC, DEF♯, E♭FG. Play the chords together and in various patterns which you feel create the right impression. Try them out on the piano with the sustaining pedal down. Listen to Debussy's Prelude *'Voiles'*.

3 Wind. Shelley in his poem 'A Dirge' describes the mournful aspect of the wind. The lamenting atmosphere of the poem lends itself well to a setting using a limited range of notes. Take, for example, the range of a fourth: from, say, C to F. Ask the children to sing these two notes and the notes between them over again several times until they are firmly in their minds; then try singing the poem within this musical range. The first two lines might turn out something like this:

Rough wind that moan - est loud   Grief too sad for   song, *etc.*

It could be accompanied by a funeral march rhythm on a bass drum:

Rough wind, that moanest loud
  Grief too sad for song;
Wild wind, when sullen cloud
  Knells all the night long;
Sad storm, whose tears are vain,
Bare woods, whose branches strain,
Deep caves and dreary main—
  Wail, for the world's wrong!

This could also be accompanied by wind sounds vocalised on various syllables, or lazy shakes of shakers filled with small objects such as seeds or sand.

4 Rain. This could be developed from the rain patterns in the storm picture, or used as an opportunity for creating patterns on the keyboard. Try starting with a pattern based on the black notes (any rhythmic pattern, using the black notes in any order, will work) or a pattern based on a triad. This is a set of three notes a third apart: for example CEG, DFA or EGB, The pattern should be simple both rhythmically and melodically so that it can be repeated easily at different pitches and with either hand. This is a simple example based on the triad:

Imagine something happening in the rain, like a girl skipping along a busy street and jumping in the puddles.

Imagine the towering buildings and play the pattern low at first, then rising higher, or in octaves spanning the whole keyboard.

Imagine the traffic hissing along the road and add this sound to the rain pattern. This could be a vocal sound, or you might use the piano to play a glissando with the thumb, or a pattern involving a chromatic scale (a scale using all the notes, black and white, one by one).

Invent a skipping tune for the girl. If this is a class activity rather than an activity by smaller groups, the class could sing this. Play the rain pattern high up and try this tune beneath it.

Use several players at one keyboard. Percussion effects could be added as well. Put the ideas together in any way you find satisfying.

Compare the final project with Debussy's 'Dr Gradus ad Parnassum' from the *Children's Corner Suite*; this is also based on an exploration of chordal patterns. There are many other studies which have been built up in this way.

5 Dew. This provides a good starting point for the exploration of small metal sounds. A passage like the following from John Clare could be illustrated with effects on glockenspiel, Indian cymbals, small cymbals, small triangles, bells and small gongs, or high metal sounds made by small pieces of piping, nails of various sizes set in a piece of wood and hit with a triangle beater, and metal containers filled with nails, ball-bearings or pins.

The dewdrops on every blade of grass are so much like silver drops that I am obliged to stoop down as I walk to see if they are pearls, and those sprinkled on the ivy-woven beds of primroses underneath the hazels, whitethorns, and maples are so like gold beads that I stooped down to feel if they were hard, but they melted from my finger. And where the dew lies on the primrose, the violet and whitethorn leaves, they are emerald and beryl, yet nothing more than the dews of the morning on the budding leaves; nay, the road grasses are covered with gold and silver beads, and the further we go the brighter they seem to shine, like solid gold and silver. It is nothing more than the sun's light and shade upon them in the dewy morning; every thorn-point and bramble spear has its trembling ornament; till the wind gets a little brisker, and then all is shaken off, and all the shining jewellery passes away into a common spring morning full of budding leaves, primroses, violets, vernal speedwell, bluebell, and orchis and commonplace objects.

Use a combination of two of the small sounds.

Use two other small sounds combined.

Use two further sounds.

Combine four of the sounds.

Combine all the sounds.

Let it rise to a crescendo and finish in a cascade of sounds.

6 November. Use Thomas Hood's poem 'No!' as the basis of a musical piece.

> No sun—no moon!
> No morn—no noon—
> No dawn—no dusk—no proper time of day—
> No sky—no earthly view
> No distance looking blue—
> No road—no street—no 't'other side the way'—
> No end to any Row
> No indications where the crescents go—
> No top to any steeple—
> No recognitions of familiar people—
> No courtesies for showing 'em—
> No knowing 'em!
> No travelling at all—no locomotion,
> No inkling of the way—no notion—
> 'No go'—by land or ocean—
> No mail—no post
> No news from any foreign court—
> No Park—no King—no afternoon gentility—
> No company—no nobility—
> No warmth, no cheerfulness, no healthful ease,
> No comfortable feel in any member—
> No shade, no shine, no butterflies, no bees,
> No fruits, no flowers, no leaves, no birds—
> November!

This is a poem with a strongly rhythmic pattern. It is dominated by the rhythm:

This rhythmic pattern could be the basis for an instrumental tune. As a starting point, a child can take four notes (DFAB♭) and play the following rhythm on them:

No sun – No moon! No morn—no noon—No dawn– no dusk—no pro-per time of day —

If one already has a rhythm it makes tune composition much easier. Children will feel the rhythm even more strongly if the poem is first used for choral speech. The child can then use this pattern as a basis for a piece, repeating it on different instruments, at different pitches, loud and soft, and so on. (This type of repeated pattern is called a *motif;* see pp. 22-23.) He could choose instruments to reflect the bleak, depressed atmosphere of the poem.

Project 7
THE RIVER

A   Ask the class to imagine a river running from its source to the sea. (This might be linked with geographical work.) Imagine the spring at the source high up in the mountains, then the little waterfalls as the stream descends to the forests and the villages where people fish in it. After that it flows into a town, through a park and then dirtily between factories and on to the docks and into the sea. Ask each child to take one aspect of the river's journey and describe it. Leave only the pentatonic scale on the pitched instruments (see p. 10) and encourage the players of these, and any recorder players, to make up a tune.

B   Choose the most successful of the tunes as the main river tune, or combine two tunes. Choose a variety of pitched instruments to play it. You might choose a small glockenspiel for the river at its source, a recorder for where it flows through the village, and the piano (in octaves) where it flows into the sea. Then, around this main tune, add other sounds the children have suggested. Rhythmic drum patterns may suggest the factories, lively tambourine patterns children's games in the park, and so on. The class could listen to Smetana's tone poem 'Vltava' which is a description of the course of the River Moldau from its source to the sea. Further ideas may also be found in Tennyson's poem 'The Brook'. This could also be linked to a movement sequence.

C   Reflections in the water have been a favourite subject for composers (such as Debussy's *Reflets dans l'eau*). This short Japanese poem by Uejima Onitsura is ideal for exploring music's potential for expressing reflection:

> A trout leaps high—
> Below him in the river bottom
> Clouds flow by.

If a good river tune has already been created as part of the previous work it can be used as the basis for this composition, with the music describing the reflections of the clouds woven around it. One can make a mirror image of a tune by tuning it upside-down (inverting it). This simply means that where the original tune went up, the inversion goes down the same distance. Thus, if this is the original tune it looks like this:

67

the upside-down version looks like this:

Taking the river tune as a basis, hold a conversation between two instruments—two glockenspiels, one high and one low, or a recorder and a glockenspiel, or any pair of melodic instruments—the second answering the first by turning the tune upside down. So the pattern visually looks like this:

Once the idea has been well grasped, a prolonged improvisation using this technique may take place; then, of course, the inversion will be more impressionistic: the distances between the notes will not be exactly the same. A complex modern composition that uses this technique is 'Narcissus' by Tristram Cary. A further composition, one dealing with clouds, is Debussy's 'Nuages' from Nocturnes.

Project 8
THE SEA

A Try to create an impression of the mystery and magic of the sea. Bring in a sea shell for the class to listen to. Describe the different moods of the sea. The children may be fascinated enough to write a poem about it, like the one written by seven-year-old Andrew Perkins:

> When the sea is calm it makes a rippling sound
> Like a strange creature underground,
> But when it is rough
> The sea is like a mad game of blind-man's-buff.
> To me the sea is fascinating and strange
> It rolls on range upon range.
> I like the sea.

This makes a good starting point for musical exploration of the different moods of the sea. The 'rippling sound' of the calm sea is often described in musical terms, as this passage from Walt Whitman shows:

> There is a dream, a picture, that for years at intervals (sometimes quite long ones, but surely again, in time), has come noiselessly up before me, and I really believe, fiction as it is, has enter'd largely into my practical life—certainly into my writings, and shaped and coloured them. It is nothing more or less than a stretch of interminable white-brown sand, hard and smooth and broad, with the ocean perpetually, grandly, rolling in upon it, with slow-measured sweep, with rustle and hiss and foam, and many a thump as of low bass drums. This scene, this picture, I say, has risen before me at times for years. Sometimes I wake at night and can hear and see it plainly.

The class will be able to draw ideas from these descriptions; they can describe the hiss with maracas and sandpaper blocks or with words containing 'sss', 'ff' or 'ssh'. Use these in the dynamic pattern:

Drum with felt beater

At the centre of this 'the thump of low bass drums' is added. Ask the children to choose one aspect of the sea—the wind, the waves, the pebbles—to describe musically.

69

B   Build these descriptions up group by group against the hissing background, or set them against a background of tape-recorded sound which suggests the vastness of the sea—a cymbal crash slowed down, for example. The order might be:

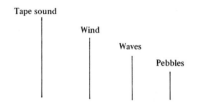

Each group of sounds continues softly until the picture is complete. You can carry on perfecting your picture, perhaps by adding the call of sea birds. The effect of vastness may be increased if you use all the space in a large room or school hall. The groups could be placed like this:

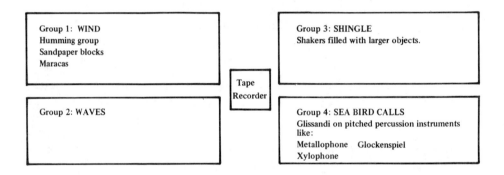

After using the sounds they have already created the children might improvise more sounds so that the effect is that of a dialogue between the elements. There are many ways of setting about this. It could be a large-scale version of the improvisation discussed on p. 22. One instrument—the piano, for example—could keep an ostinato pattern going to hold it all together. The groups could use each of their instruments singly or in pairs; it is difficult for a large group of instruments to improvise simultaneously. The sequence of instruments should be worked out carefully beforehand. If each group worked quite independently at first until it has produced some good material, it could then get together with another group and see how to relate the material of one to the other (by inversion: p. 22; by canon: p. 19, transferring the other group's ideas to their own instruments, and so forth).

Listen to Debussy's *La Mer*.

C   1   Use this poem by Longfellow as the basis of a musical composition. It takes the theme of rising and falling and could follow the dynamic pattern sketched by the side. The chorus line itself obviously lends itself to the ⊂===⊃ dynamic pattern.

The tide rises, the tide falls,
The twilight darkens, the curlew calls;
Along the sea-sands damp and brown
The traveller hastens toward the town,
  And the tide rises, the tide falls.

Darkness settles on roofs and walls,
But the sea in the darkness calls and calls;
The little waves, with their soft white hands,
Efface the footprints in the sands,
  And the tide rises, the tide falls.

The morning breaks; the steeds in their stalls
Stamp and neigh, as the hostler calls;
The day returns, but nevermore
Returns the traveller to the shore,
  And the tide rises, the tide falls.

2   Sailors. The historical aspect can be explored. Sea shanties can be linked with
ships of various periods and famous sea battles (for example, 'Boney was a warrior').
Children can add their own verses to shanties, much in the way that the shanty-man
would have done. (The shanty-man was the sailor who sang the verses alone; the other
sailors joined in the chorus):

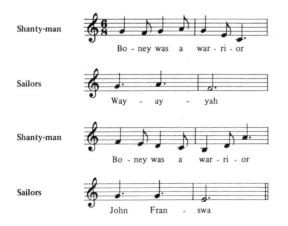

There are a number of original verses to this but it would be quite simple to make up
new verses from a basic knowledge of Napoleon (although the original did not keep
very closely to a historically accurate account of his life and exploits!) The shanty-man
probably made up some of the words as he went along, using witty topical verses to
liven up the sailors' monotonous tasks. 'Boney was a warrior' is an example of a
halliard shanty, used for hauling the ropes which pulled the sails up, a task which

required short pulls. Fore-sheet shanties, however, were sung when the other sails were already up and to hoist the fore-sheet the men had to give only one long pull:

We'll haul on the bow-lin, so ear-ly in the morn - ing, We'll haul on the bow-lin, the bow-lin, Haul!

These shanties are not the only songs of the sea; there were also sea-songs used for relaxation and recreation. Some retained the strong rhythms of the shanties, but others had gentler, less repetitive rhythms. There are a number of books of and about shanties; it is a huge subject. The most authoritative and detailed is Stan Hugill's *Shanties of the Seven Seas* (Routledge and Kegan Paul) and a very readable simple introduction is *Sailors' Songs and Shanties* by Michael Hurd (Oxford University Press). Shanties could be used in class as the basis of a drama about the sea.

3   Ships. Again, this could be linked with historical and geographical studies. Ships have inspired many composers; Debussy's *En Bateau* and Mendelssohn's *Calm Sea and Prosperous Voyage* are but two examples. Walton's *Portsmouth Point* would be a very useful starting point for a dance-drama about life in a port. Variation 13 of Elgar's *Enigma Variations* describes a lady who was on a sea voyage when he composed the piece; for this, he not only included a quotation from Mendelssohn's *Calm Sea and Prosperous Voyage,* but also the sound of the sea and the chug of the engines. The combination of these two sounds is well expressed in the following passage written by Joseph Conrad. It could be the basis of a composition concerned primarily with silence, as its opening suggests, with small sounds being placed one by one in the 'container' of silence. It could also be linked with the experience of lone yachtsmen like Sir Francis Chichester, or with space flight (bearing in mind, however, that space is a vacuum and sound will not travel through it).

A marvellous stillness pervaded the world, and the stars, together with the serenity of their rays, seemed to shed upon the earth the assurance of everlasting security. The young moon, recurved, and shining low in the west, was like a slender shaving thrown up from a bar of gold, and the Arabian Sea, smooth and cool to the eye like a sheet of ice, extended its perfect level to the perfect circle of a dark horizon. The propeller turned without a check, as though its beat had been part of the scheme of a safe universe; and on each side of the Patna two deep folds of water, permanent and sombre on the unwrinkled shimmer, enclosed within their straight and diverging ridges a few white swirls of foam bursting in a low

Gold: snatch of melody in an arch shape.
A very smooth pattern on the metallophone: of limited range, slow moving.
Drum-beat.

Interpret this pattern in musical sounds: perhaps the swirls on soft tambourines, and the two lines with a glissando on two glockenspiels (perhaps one running up and the other down).

hiss, a few wavelets, a few ripples, a few undulations that, left behind, agitated the surface of the sea for an instant after the passage of the ship, subsided splashing gently, calmed down at last into the circular stillness of water and sky with the black speck of the moving hull remaining everlasting in its centre.	Hiss of shakers and sandpaper. Small tambourine shakes. Use the shakers and maracas and perhaps a cymbal with a wire brush.

The effect of the final composition is probably better if the passage is not read at the same time. The composition could be held together with the very soft sound of the engines, either as a muffled drum beat or as a spoken group activity:

Speaker A: Hmm ——————————
Speaker B: Ssh – Ssh – Ssh – Ssh
Speaker C: Ticka - tacka – ticka - tacka

4 Travel. This is the source of a great deal of the sea's magic. Use an atlas to find the names of some exotic places, then use them as the basis for a composition like the sea compositions in the first chapter (see pp. 7-9). Some examples of suitable names: Popocatopetl, Morocco, Salt Lake City, Ethiopia, Tien Shan, Serengeti, Madagascar, Kilimanjaro, Sahara, Tanzania, Mozambique. Compare the results of your experiment with Toch's 'Geographical Fugue' (Mills Music).

5 Explore some of the legends associated with the sea. You could use the stories of cities swallowed up by the waves as the basis for a music and drama project and follow it up by listening to Debussy's 'Submerged Cathedral'. Listen to Wagner's opera *The Flying Dutchman*, which has a particularly descriptive overture.

Project 9
MACHINERY

A   Discuss rhythmic and arhythmic sounds. (Many of the previous projects have been concerned with sounds without clearly defined rhythms.) Ask the children to imagine machine noises. You can use tape recordings of real machines or arrange for the children to visit places where they will hear machinery working. It will be quite easy for them to listen to domestic machinery—electric mixers, washing machines, vacuum cleaners—and traffic noises. Then ask each child to make up a sound that can be associated with a particular machine, either a rhythmic sound or a continuous sound like a hum or a whirr. Word sounds can be used as well—*mm, ch-ssh,* and so forth.

B   Divide the children into groups of four so that they can make up a combined machine noise from their separate sounds. Discuss which kinds of sounds might combine well together. Then bring all the groups together to make a sequence of noises for a machine with several processes, like a washing machine. (This could also be linked with movement, and with the invention of imaginery machines in craft classes.)

C   **1**   Make a machine noise from exclusively vocal sounds, for example:

1st Person :	Mm _
2nd Person:	Chssh _ _ _ Chssh _ _ _ Chssh _ _ _ Chssh _ _ _ Chssh _ _ _ Chssh _ _ _ _ _
3rd Person:	Pippi ppi ppi ppi ppi ppi ppi ppi ppi ppi ppi ppi ppi ppi ppi ppi ppi ppi ppi ppi ppi ppi ppi
4th Person:	Bong (ng) _ _ _ _ _ _ _ _ _ _ _ _ Bong (ng) _ _ _ _ _ _ _ _ _ _ _ _ _

2   Make up a composition of clock sounds. Let each child choose a type of clock, and decide on the pitch and quality of the tick, the speed, and perhaps the chime. Try it out vocally or instrumentally. (Unusual instruments may be useful here: cutlery, stones, wooden or plastic objects hit together.) Then try blending some of the rhythms together; this should be approached gradually, as it will not be easy. The final effect will be that of polyrhythm (many different rhythms playing one against the other; see p. 16). A polyrhythmic composition provides good practice for holding one's own rhythmic pattern against the others.

3   Make a collection of taped machine noises. Encourage the children to be resourceful and tape such things as mechanical toys, musical boxes, lawn mowers and so on. Try to arrange a visit to a local factory or farm and take a tape recorder along. This might lead to a discussion of the life of people who work continually in this noise and the effect it has on them. By editing your tape collection you could construct a piece called 'Machines'. You will find that some of the sounds will be even more exciting if they are speeded up or slowed down (see p. 31).

4 Make a toy (listen to Tom Paxton's song 'The Marvelous Toy') in craft and invent movements for it in dance, using some mechanical percussion sounds combined with a tune on the xylophone.

5 Look at some of the songs of the industrial revolution like 'Fourpence a Day' and others from *The Singing Island* (Mills Music). Try making up a ballad for a modern factory worker, using the information gathered when collecting factory sounds. Such a ballad might begin like this:

> I rise at six each working day
>   And set out in my car;
> Through rush- hour crowds I thread my way;
>   The factory's not far.

Try setting your own ballad to a simple tune. One way of creating a tune is by playing a chord sequence over again and again until a tune emerges from it (see p. 25). Decide where the bars or stresses should fall in the first verse; for example:

> I/rise at six each/working day
>   And/set out in my/car;
> Through/rush-hour crowds I/thread my way;
>   The/factory's not/far.

This needs a chord sequence spread over eight bars. Choose a sequence of eight chords, experimenting on piano or guitar or even chime bars in any key that is easy: e.g. G major (GBD), E Minor (EGB) C major (CEG), E Minor (EGB) A minor (ACE), B minor (BDF♯), C major (CEG) or G major (GBD). The chords should be played over on the most suitable instrument while the words are chanted in rhythm; when the chord sequence is firmly in the mind, the tune can be attempted accompanied by the chordal instrument. The tune can be improvised vocally or instrumentally, although the latter is more difficult and demands some technical expertise on the part of the improviser. Here is a simple melody created in this way:

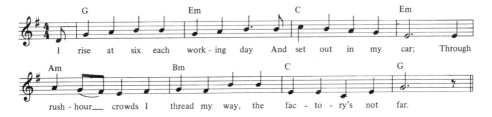

Project 10
THE ANIMAL WORLD

A   Talk about the way in which various animals move—how bulls and buffaloes charge, how frogs and kangaroos hop, how horses and deer leap, and so on. Ask each child to look at his instrument and find out what shape of tune and what type of rhythm it can play easily. For example, for animals that leap, such as horses, stags and rabbits, a variety of leaping tunes can be invented. One might have really big slow leaps, others smaller leaps in jagged or smooth rhythms. These three very simple examples show this:

If you keep the same note at the bottom of each jump, as here, your tunes are more likely to fit together satisfactorily and are easier to play.

Frogs hopping could be suggested by playing a scraper followed by a whip or wood-block:

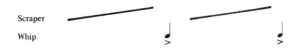

Or a tune that rises gradually and drops suddenly, like this:

This may well have been invented at the piano, on which it is easy to play upward runs of five notes and leaps. The lower note of the leap could be reinforced by a low drum-beat.

76

For animals that charge, one might use a very simple roll on a drum, rising and falling:

Drum Roll

More ambitious would be a smooth tune moving mostly by steps—at its simplest a scale-pattern:

For animals that scurry, like mice and rats, try steadily rhythmic rustling sounds, some fast and some slow. Suitable instruments would be maracas, sandpaper blocks, or scratching the surface of a drum with a finger or sandpaper. One low tune or several low tunes of differing speeds could be used.

For kangaroos hopping, a gentle tune with big leaps would be appropriate:

Try this on an instrument that can play a good staccato, like the xylophone or piano.

B   Either **1** Make a set of pieces in which each handles a different kind of movement. For example: frogs and kangaroos; buffaloes and bison; mice, rats, beavers and badgers; cats, wolves and stoats.

Or **2** Work in pairs, creating a dialogue between two very contrasted creatures, for example: the elephant and the butterfly; the mouse and the lion; the frog and the cat.

Or **3** Compose a piece called 'Man the Invader'. Imagine a man walking through a wood, portrayed by a heavy drum beat, and set against this the musical patterns of the different animals he disturbs.

C   **1**   Use 'The Night Song of the Fish' by Christian Morgenstern as the basis for a composition. This poem can probably be played on instruments more easily than it can be read in words.

There may well be as many interpretations as children in the class. The lines might be long notes from a chime bar and the curved lines might be short glissandi up and down a glockenspiel. There could be a pause at the end of each line, or the lines could be read in pairs so that the lined and curved notes alternate. The long notes and glissandi could be played on different instruments for variety, returning to the original instruments at the end. The curves might also be interpreted as scrapes up and down a scraper, and the long notes as beats on a tambour. The possibilities are endless.

2 Birds are a favourite subject with composers. Shelley's 'A Widow Bird' has an atmosphere that could be perfectly captured by an ostinato on a metal pitched instrument such as a glockenspiel, perhaps combined with a triangle to produce the icy effect. This could be used as the accompaniment to the poem set as a song using the pentatonic scale (see p. 10). A suggested simple ostinato is the following:

A widow bird sate mourning for her love
Upon a wintry bough;
The frozen wind crept on above,
The freezing stream below.

There was no leaf upon the forest bare,
No flower upon the ground,
And little motion in the air
Except the mill-wheel's sound.

3 Use two coconut shells to make the sound of horses' hooves, and make up a story of a rider setting out across the hills, passing by mountain streams and through forests on his way to a village.

4 There are many pieces of music which were inspired by the animal world. These are just a few listening suggestions:

Saint-Saens	'The Carnival of the Animals'
Vaughan Williams	'The Lark Ascending'
Jacques Ibert	'The Little White Donkey'
Rimsky Korsakov	'The Flight of the Bumble Bee'
Delius	'On Hearing the First Cuckoo in Spring'.

Project 11
SILENCE

A An increasing number of people in the musical and educational world think that music teaching in today's world should be more concerned with silence than with increasing the already large range of sound-making devices. Start the project with a silence survey. If possible, organize the lesson so that you do not need to speak at all. Write the instructions on the blackboard, and let the class sit in silence and note down all the sounds they can hear in the 'silence' around them. They could list them under the headings 'sounds made by me', 'sounds made by other people in the room', 'sounds outside the room'. Children unable to write could draw them. Ask if they heard such sounds as their own breathing and the rustle of their own clothing. Discuss whether there is such a thing as silence anywhere. Ask them to listen for silence at home and report back with their findings. Did they find it? Where? How near did they get to it? What sounds prevented them from finding it?

B Ask each child to invent or bring with him from home things that make the smallest sound he can find. Arrange them in an order. Tell the children that you are going to put their sounds one by one into little pockets of silence. Ask them to make their sounds at five-second intervals; either use a clock with a second hand that is visible to all or give signals to the class with your hand. Each of them should make his sound and then leave the rest of the five seconds silent. This exercise can create quite a magical atmosphere in the class-room.

C **1** Build up a musical composition using shakers of various materials (plastic, wood, metal, cardboard, papier mâché) containing different sizes of filling material (seeds, ball-bearings, salt, rice, sand, stones). Set these shaker sounds in pockets of silence.

2 Use this poem about autumn by an unknown poet as the basis for a composition, using rustling sounds to suggest the dryness of autumn leaves and the fruits hanging on the trees. Leaves, various types of paper (greaseproof, tissue, cellophane) and bundles of twigs all have different qualities of sound, and they are small sounds that demand careful listening if one is to distinguish between them. Maraca sounds (containers with various materials in them; see p. 35) and sounds made by a wire brush on drums, cymbals and tambourines could be added as well:

> There are nuts on the trees,
>   In their clusters of brown,
> And the leaves are like butterflies,
>   Fluttering down;
> The cornfields are golden,
>   The sunlight is clear,
> And the apples are rosy
> Now Autumn is here.

79

This might be followed by examining the folk customs associated with harvest time. It was traditionally a time for celebration. The English Folk Dance and Song Society—Cecil Sharp House, 2 Regent's Park Road, London NW1—will supply further information. *Frost and Fire*, a record by the Watersons (Topic 12T36), includes some of the songs associated with autumn as well as others showing how the ceremonies of pre-Christian religion were linked with the seasons of the year.

3 Rustling sounds could be organised into an ostinato pattern in a composition inspired by this passage from Dorothy Wordsworth's Journals:

'The Coleridges left us. A cold windy morning. Walked with them half way. On our return, sheltered under the hollies, during a hail-shower. The withered leaves danced with the hailstorm. William wrote a description of the storm.'

The rustle pattern could at first have many rests in it:

Having played the pattern once, notes on the metal instrument—either pitched (like a glockenspiel) or unpitched (like a triangle)—can be added in place of the rests. A dancing tune for the withered leaves could be gradually introduced (a $\frac{6}{8}$ jig tune might be appropriate) above the rustles, and more rustles could be introduced to fill in all the rests. At the end the original pattern could be restored.

4 Use this description of the peace and stillness of a winter wood (also by Dorothy Wordsworth) as the basis of a composition about silence, broken only by the smallest sounds suggested by the ideas in the passage. The periods of silence could be quite long. The second hand of a clock might help with the timing, as suggested at the beginning of the project. (This passage could even be used to inspire the start of the whole project on silence.)

A deep snow upon the ground. William and Coleridge walked to Mr Bartholomew's, and to Stowey. William returned, and we walked through the wood into the Coombe to fetch some eggs. The sun shone bright and clear. A deep stillness in the thickest part of the wood, undisturbed except by the occasional dropping of the snow from the holly boughs;

Use a small paper rustle like tissue paper. Use small glissandi on the glockenspiel.

no other sound but that of the water,

Use a tune or pattern on a descant recorder.

and the slender notes of a redbreast, which sang at intervals on the outskirts of the southern side of the wood. There the bright green moss was bare at the roots of the trees, and the little birds were upon it. The whole appearance of the wood was enchanting; and each tree, taken singly, was beautiful.

Use a sound to represent each tree. (It may be a 'tree-shaped' tune—one that rises and falls.)

The branches of the hollies pendent with
their white burden, but still showing their
bright red berries, and their glossy green | Play a pattern representing the holly
leaves. The bare branches of the oaks | berries, perhaps on a triangle.
thickened by the snow. | A scraper might suggest the branches.

This is one composition that should certainly be performed alone rather than while the passage is being read. The sounds taken from the passage could easily be reorganised and reused as part of a musical pattern. For example, paper rustles suggesting the snow falling could be used between the various other sounds (giving a rondo structure—ABACADA—as discussed on p. 16). The children should never forget, however, that composition is basically about silence and that the 'rests' are more important than the sounds themselves.

5 Follow up your investigation into the sounds that make up silence today by looking at the difference between the sounds of the twentieth century and those of previous centuries. Take a photograph of a busy city scene and, say, one of Breughel's busier paintings, and make a list of all the sounds represented in each scene. Then compose a musical description for each. The modern one could consist of tape recordings made by the class and edited into an interesting order. You might also be able to find poems dealing with the nature of silence in the country and in the town. This might lead to a discussion of the children's fears (if any) about silence of different kinds.

Project 12
THE MONKEYS: a story by Grete Fischer

A Experiment with rhythmic canon (each part having the same rhythm but starting at a
different time, see p. 19). If you keep increasing the number of instruments a good
climax will be reached. Ask each child to invent an aggressive rhythm, then set the
class to work in pairs, each pair choosing one of their two rhythms and using it in
canon like this:

1st part: ♫ ♩ ♫ ♩ ♩ ♩ ♪♫ ♩ ♫ ♩

2nd part: ♫ ♩ ♫ ♩ ♩ ♪♫ ♩ *etc.*

Next set them to work in fours and experiment with increasing the number of
instruments to build up a climax. Two groups could then combine, each group
retaining its own rhythm, and try combining the two rhythms to produce a double
canon. Both groups could start at the same time, or one group could begin first and the
other group join them gradually, so that the second group will finish after the first
group.

B Read the monkey story to the children. To do this, follow the parts of the three
narrators in the worked-out version in section C. Discuss the use of the music with the
children. Then decide on a rhythmic pattern for Naagu and Nuugu. These could be
two good rhythms from the work done in section A.

C Prepare a performance of the story with musical accompaniment. This might be
presented by two opposing groups of people—speakers and instrumentalists
—perhaps placed at either side of a stage. Each group should have its own main
speaker and there should also be one main narrating speaker independent of the
groups. Each group must have its own collection of instruments—all of a menacing,
dark kind but of differing tone colours. In this version, Naagu's group has bongo
drums, wood-box, tambourine, maracas and xylophone, and Nuugu's group a
medium-sized tambour struck with a padded stick, claves, a cymbal (preferably the
suspended type) struck either with wire brushes or padded sticks, and a scraper and
metallophone. The overriding atmosphere of war might be set by playing a steady beat
on a bass drum which continues all the way through, except perhaps during the last
paragraph. Each group can have its own rhythmic pattern; both aggressive, but
contrasted. The suggested rhythms for this version are

♩ ♩ ♩ ♫ ♫♫ ♩ ♩

for Naagu and

𝅗𝅥 𝅗𝅥 ♪𝅗𝅥. 𝅗𝅥

for Nuugu. Naagu's faster pattern is more suited to the instruments in his group, Nuugu's instruments having the sustaining power necessary for his pattern, which includes much longer notes.

These suggestions follow up the children's early experiments with canon and with creating a sense of climax by using a build-up of instruments. This project also uses contrasted rhythms to create the idea of conflict. If it is used with the whole class, the children should choose their rhythms and instruments under a teacher's guidance.

THE MONKEYS

NARRATOR	NAAGU'S GROUP — Narrator	NAAGU'S GROUP — Music	NUUGU'S GROUP — Music	NUUGU'S GROUP — Narrator
Two tribes of monkeys lived in the jungle not far from each other. They more or less respected each other's area. Each tribe had a leader, the eldest and strongest of the herd. One was called	Naagu.			
The other's name was				Nuugu.
	One day, Naagu was sitting in a tree a little apart from his family and servants, when he spotted Nuugu in a big tree just opposite.	*Play pattern once on bongos:* ♩ ♩ ♫ , ♫ ♫ ♩ ♩ ᵢ	*Play pattern on tambour:* ♩ ♩ ♩ ♪ ♩· ♩ ᵢ	
		Play pattern once.	*Play pattern again.*	Nuugu saw him too.
And they started shouting at each other, more in play than in earnest, as monkeys do.	"You beast" shouted Naagu, and added a few more words of the same kind.	*Play pattern.*	*Play pattern.*	"You ugly brute" shouted Nuugu, happily.
And so they went on.		*Play the patterns together twice, softly.*		

	NAAGU'S GROUP			NUUGU'S GROUP	
NARRATOR	Narrator	Music		Music	Narrator
					Nuugu retaliated.
		Play the pattern on the wood-box, repeating it for as long as this line lasts.		*Play the pattern on the claves and repeat it for as long as this line lasts.*	
					A stick hit Nuugu's nose and he shouted "You brute! You dare to hit me and I shall bash your nose in!"
				Play the pattern in canon on claves and tambour for as long as this line lasts.	
And the two began bombarding each other with fruit and sticks. By and by they got hotter and hotter.	But after a while Nuugu used a word which stung. Naagu got cross, picked up a nut and threw it at Nuugu.				
By that time Naagu's women and the other apes had come nearer and watched the quarrel. Now they started to chatter and scream and pushed nearer and shouted in Naagu's ear:	"Have you heard? Have you heard him? He wants to bash your nose in! You can't let him bash your nose in! You go in first— you bash his nose in!" They screamed and pushed and Naagu got almost dizzy and very angry, so he jumped forward and bashed Nuugu's nose in.	*This could be spoken in canon, the speech being accompanied by Naagu's rhythm in canon on bongos and wood-box.*			
		Rhythms suddenly stop.			

NARRATOR	NAAGU'S GROUP		Music	NUUGU'S GROUP
	Narrator	*Music*		*Narrator*
				Nuugu howled with pain, half blind with blood running from his nose, and he just had time to hit back and smash Naagu's nose.
	Naagu jumped back to his own tree, whining and bleeding.	*Play Naagu's pattern once slowly and softly on the bongos.* *Play Naagu's rhythm in canon as before, on wood-box and bongos.*	*Rhythms stop.*	
The whole tribe was up and furiously shouting around him and his ears were ringing with their comments.				
	"Look what he has done to you! Look, he'll do it again! Don't let him do it again! You hit him first— that will teach him! Hit him! Hit him!"	*One of these phrases can be chosen and said in canon:*		

1st Group He'll do it a-gain, He'll do it etc

2nd Group He'll do it a – gain etc

NARRATOR	NAAGU'S GROUP		Music	NUUGU'S GROUP
			Resume Nuugu's pattern in canon on claves and tambour. Choose one of the phrases in the speech and say it in canon.	Nuugu's tribe made the same noise, the trees were filled with their cries. "Nuugu! Look what he has done to you! He's wicked! He'll do it again! He has bashed your nose— go and bite off his ear!" Nuugu, still nursing his wound, hesitated.
	But Naagu's tribe had heard the threat and they bellowed with anger.	*Play pattern once loudly on bongos, wood-box and tambourine.*	*Play Naagu's rhythm slowly once.*	

NARRATOR	Naagu's Group — Narrator	Naagu's Group — Music	Nuugu's Group — Music	Nuugu's Group — Narrator
			Play the pattern once loudly on tambour, claves and cymbal.	"You wait! I'll tear your ear off" screamed Nuugu. "Bravo!" shouted his followers, "You do that! Teach him a lesson!"
	But Naagu's tribe had heard it and they shouted back "Go! Go! Go! Go! Bite his ear off or he will do it first!" So Naagu jumped forward and bit Nuugu's ear off.	*Play the rhythm in three-part canon on bongos, wood-box and tambourine.* [music notation]		
			Play pattern in three-part canon on tambour, claves and cymbals: [music notation]	Nuugu screamed and all his followers joined in. "My ear! My ear!" wailed Nuugu. "You've bitten my ear off! I'll poke your eye out, I will."
	Naagu heard the threat with horror. He would have liked to back out; but all the other apes gathered around him and spurred him on: "Will you risk your eyes? You are stronger than he is, you're a hero! You've bitten his ear off, now go for his eyes!"	*Play the pattern once slowly on bongo.* *Play the pattern in four-part canon on bongos, wood-box, tambourine and maracas.*		
			Play pattern more loudly on tambour, claves, cymbal and scraper.	At that moment Nuugu jumped, Naagu covered his eyes, Nuugu bit his ear off and jumped back.

87

NARRATOR   Narrator   Music   NAAGU'S GROUP   Music   NUUGU'S GROUP   Narrator

Now both were bleeding from nose and ear and both were furious.

Deafened by the noise his followers made, Naagu thought only of revenge. He saw Nuugu crouching to jump again and to forestall him at all costs he moved first and really poked Nuugu's right eye out. But he had no time to get back to his own tree.

Put the two patterns against one another, each one being played on all available instruments. A tune can be made up for each animal, and the xylophone can be added to Naagu's group and the metallophone to Nuugu's.

Keeping the two rhythms going against one another, play Naagu's in canon on his instruments, and Nuugu's in canon on his instruments, so that the final effect is as below:

Bongos
Woodbox
Tambourine
Maracas and Xylophone
Tambour
Claves
Cymbal
Scraper and Metallophone

Blinded and senseless with pain, Nuugu seized him and pressed his thumbs in both his eyes.

NARRATOR	NAAGU'S GROUP		NUUGU'S GROUP	
	Narrator	*Music*	*Music*	*Narrator*
				"Tear his guts out! Finish him off! Make him pay!"
	"Tear his guts out! Finish him off! Make him pay!"	*Let the music rise to a crescendo, with the words being shouted over the top of it.*		
The other apes screamed out:				
Nuugu and Naagu fell out of the tree. Still tearing at each other, they lay on the ground, bleeding and wailing and ready to die.		*Let the music drop in volume and the instruments drop out one by one, until only the two pitched ones are left.*		
Then they fell silent. Then Nuugu said:		*Silence - - - - - - - - - - -*	*Silence - - - - - - - - - - -*	
			Play pattern slowly on xylophone.	"Can you remember what we were fighting for?"
	"No" said Naagu. "do you know who started it?"	*Play pattern slowly on xylophone.*		
			Play pattern slowly on metallophone.	"No and I don't care" said Nuugu.
	"We might just as well make peace," said Naagu.	*Play pattern slowly on metallophone.*		
And they died.		*Play patterns slowly together on pitched instruments.*		
		Silence - - - - - - - - - - -		
That's how the apes make war.				

Project 13
THE WEEDS

A Read the story to the children and discuss the places at which music might be appropriate. Work on each musical unit separately as a class. Work at the music and movement simultaneously where this is possible, so that the two aspects interact. These are the units suggested in the worked-out scheme in section C.

1 Musical Introduction—A Garden.
Either (a) Ask each child to choose a flower and paint it musically, choosing a suitable instrument. Then play the compositions one after another or choose a few and combine them.
Or (b) Choose the names of various flowers, including weeds, and transfer the word rhythms to suitable instruments. You can combine these in the same way that the names of different seas were combined in the setting of Psalm 93 in Chapter 1 (see pp. 7-8).

2 Rain Shower. How do rain showers start? How do they finish? How strong is this one going to be? Who has an instrument suitable for starting the storm? Take one of the better flower tunes and against it play the pattern of the rain (perhaps simply a repeated note on a glockenspiel, or glasses hit with a metal beater). Build up the storm pattern, making sure that any smaller sounds suggested (such as raindrops) enter near the beginning, and that the end is as satisfactory as the beginning.

3 Dialogue between Robin and his father. Divide the class into two groups, one group to portray Robin and the other, his father. Try to make two really contrasted rhythms (rather than tunes) for the two characters. Use these rhythms separately at first, gradually bringing them closer together until they are used simultaneously. For example:

Choose a suitable instrument for each character. These might be changed during the course of the argument.

4 Sleep music or falling asleep.
Either (a) This might take the form of a melody (rather than just a rhythm) played on an instrument capable of producing a smooth line, like a recorder.
Or (b) This might be a simple scale (perhaps pentatonic) played on a glockenspiel accompanied by unpitched sounds decreasing in volume. Once you have completed this, it might be compared with Schumann's 'Child falling asleep' from *Scenes from Childhood,* or with both traditional and composed lullabies.

5 The Battle of the Roots. This could be done by setting up two contrasted rhythms for the two groups of weeds and the rose root. The contrast between the weed groups could be heightened by the type of instruments used:

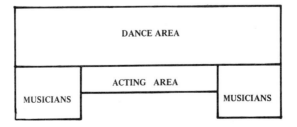

The rose root pattern needs careful thought. It could be played on a high or bright-sounding instrument, or it could even be a melody as a contrast to the plain rhythm of the groups of weeds. Here is a suggested rhythm:

This must stand out clearly, so keep the tune high and play the other rhythms on quite different and darker-sounding instruments.

B Polish up these units created in class, working in separate groups.

C Put the story together. The suggestions here combine dance, drama, mime and music. Here is a suggested layout for the final performance:

```
+--------------------------------------------------+
|                                                  |
|                  DANCE AREA                      |
|                                                  |
+----------+----------------------------+----------+
|          |        ACTING   AREA       |          |
| MUSICIANS|                            | MUSICIANS|
|          |                            |          |
+----------+----------------------------+----------+
```

These are the actors and dancers: Robin; his father; the Roots Group A; the Roots Group B; the Rose Root.

THE WEEDS

NARRATOR	MUSIC	DANCE
Robin and his father lived in a house with a fine garden.	Musical Introduction—The Garden.	
One day there was a shower of rain.	Rain Shower.	
Drama: Dialogue between father and Robin in which Robin is asked to help with the weeding. It is easy work as the soil is soft. Robin looks at the weeds which he has to pull up and he finds they are nice plants, almost as nice as the flower seedlings and much nicer than the vegetables. He is sorry for the daisies and buttercups, dandelions and milkweed: "Why, they have as much right to grow as the roses. Only because we like roses better and because we want to eat vegetables (and I don't like carrots, turnips and spinach)—we go and kill tender things." Argument with father, who thinks he is too lazy.		
Robin, however, was quite serious about it, and so he was let off and he went into a corner in the garden under the lilac bush and went to sleep.		
In his sleep Robin thought he heard a noise	Sleep Music. Keep some aspect of the sleep music going—perhaps a rhythm on a xylophone—while the narrator says these lines:	
and in his dream the noise became louder and louder, like pushing, falling, tearing and shouts and screams, as if on a battlefield.	Sudden but soft beat on tambour and/or scrape on scraper.	
	Scrape and beat become louder but the rhythm stays steady. Make sure that it has not grown so loud that the narrator is inaudible.	
He bent down to hear where the noise came from, and suddenly the soil was clear like glass, and he could see right through it.		
What he saw scared him stiff.	Glissando on a glockenspiel abruptly stops the rhythm above.	

NARRATOR	MUSIC	DANCE
	One rhythm is set up to portray Group A of the roots.	Group A of the roots start moving slowly towards Group B with twisting, twining movements around each other and stretching towards Group B.
	[musical notation]	Group B start in similar manner, gradually meeting and intermingling with Group A.
	Group B rhythm (contrasted in the quality of instruments used) starts. (Group A's rhythm should be softer here to allow it to be heard.)	
	[musical notation]	
The roots of all the plants were fighting for space and water. It looked a cruel, relentless struggle. Each of the tender little things stretched long winding arms like tentacles in all directions and pushed others aside.		
One root looked finer and somehow nobler than the others,	The rose root pattern is introduced.	One dancer (the rose root) is clearly becoming the main centre of attention among the two groups.
but it was furiously attacked by bunches of vicious creatures which tied themselves around it and choked it.	Gradually the rose root music sinks to the same level as the rhythms playing above it. (It might gradually be transposed lower and lower, or it might simply be made increasingly softer by reducing the numbers of instruments playing the melody one by one.)	The rose root is gradually overcome by the others.
"Help me!" called the root, and Robin stretched out his hand to free it.	A sudden new sound should penetrate the texture, such as a large tambour or a glissando on several glockenspiels; then the sound ceases.	As Robin stretches out a hand, all the dancers scatter in confusion.
Drama: Robin wakes up and looks in his hand and discovers he is holding some innocent-looking weeds which grow under a rose bush. As he tries to pull them up he discovers their roots are so long and tough that he can hardly	believe it. 'If the weeds have a right to live so have the roses. And if I did not check the weeds, the nobler plants could not grow at all.' [*Note*: If this is being performed as a story only, during the last speech there could be a repeat of the themes from the central drama.]	

Project 14
THE LONG LONG SPOONS

A First read the story to the children and discuss the places where music would be appropriate. Then work on the main musical sections in class. These are the units suggested in the worked-out scheme in Section C:

1 Eastern Overture.
Either (a) Use words suggesting Eastern ideas or even words from an Eastern language to build up a composition.
Or (b) Study one Eastern country in detail and then ask the class to make up a piece reflecting the mood they have caught from their studies of the country.

2 Dead March. What sort of music do we associate with death? Is it to be sad or joyful? (In light of the fact that the March to Paradise which follows this piece is probably going to be triumphant, a portrayal of the grief of the bereaved relations may be aesthetically better here.) Discuss which instruments have traditionally been associated with death—muffled drums, etc. Listen to Handel's 'Dead March in Saul'; the slow movement of Beethoven's 'Eroica' Symphony; the 'purple' movement of Bliss's *Colour Symphony*; Grieg's 'The Death of Ase'.

3 March to Paradise. Listen to and discuss various types of marches. What sort should this one be? What are the characteristics of a march? One instrument will probably have to keep a steady beat going to give it a march-like character. The exact choice of other instruments will depend on the particular character decided on for the march. If it is to be grand and triumphal, a marching tune for recorders could be composed, or a martial tune performed by recorders, such as one of Purcell's trumpet tunes. If it is to be sad and slow, wooden instruments like xylophones and wood-blocks could represent the footsteps of Ali: perhaps even frightened, rather unwilling ones.

4 Dialogue between Ali and the Guardian.
Either (a) Discuss what Ali and the guardian are like and choose an instrument to represent each of them, or make up a tune for each character. The tune could be played on a variety of instruments depending on the nature of the situation. For example, the guardian might appear severe at first, with his tune on a dark instrument like a xylophone; as he appears kinder, it could be transferred to a brighter instrument like a glockenspiel. When each character speaks, you can either modify his own tune to fit his words or speak the words above the instrumental tunes.
Or (b) Improvised Song. While the lowest instrument plays two notes in a steady pattern, two children should make up tunes to fit the various sentences as they go

along, trying to keep the expression of the words (see p. 18). This could lead to a discussion of 'question and answer' melodies and melodic shape. The children may not wish to improvise for the final performance, in which case the improvisations can be tape recorded or turned into polished tunes.

5 The Light-filled Hall. This can be taken from earlier work on the Light Project or can be an extension of some of the ideas suggested in that project. You will probably need a collection of smaller sounds and larger sounds. You can either decide on the nature of the light first and then select the appropriate sounds to use, or start by playing the smaller sounds and gradually adding the larger ones.

6 The Food. Build up a sound picture by using the word-rhythms of the names of the class's favourite dishes, or exotic dishes that they would like to try.

7 The Discontented Spirits. Let each child create a sound that suggests unhappiness and then build them all together; or use words which you feel have a dark turbulent sound, such as those with an 'oo' in them: *brooding, duly, unruly* (see p. 15).

8 The Happy Spirits. Either ask each child to create a sound which suggests happiness, and then build them all together; or use words which you feel have a 'joyful sound, such as ones that have a short 'a' sound in them; *pat, ratatat, paddle.*

B   Polish all these units in small groups.

C   Put the whole story together, adding any smaller musical interpolations the children think necessary. It could be left simply as a narrated story with musical accompaniment or it might be turned into a puppet or shadow play.

THE LONG LONG SPOONS

SPEECH	MUSIC

Narrator:
This is a legend from the East.

Use either your Eastern Overture or a recording of music from the East, such as Indian sitar music; or invent an Eastern dance for the puppets and create music especially for this.

Ali had died.

Dead March.

He went up to the doors of Paradise.

March to Paradise.

When he arrived there, the guardian stopped him

Beat on tambour.

and enquired who

An upward-turning phrase on a glockenspiel (or whichever instrument has been chosen for the guardian)—a question phrase:

and where

Another question phrase.

and what
So as to decide if he might be admitted. Ali answered all the questions.

Another question phrase (or the same one).

Here follows the dialogue between Ali and the Guardian. To allow for whichever treatment has been decided on in section A, only the text of the story is printed here.

Guardian:
Well, it seems you have been neither good nor bad. We shall give you the benefit of the doubt, and you may choose your own Paradise.

Ali:
What is my chance? What kind of Paradise is there to choose?

Guardian:
There is the Paradise of the good people and that of the bad. You see the two doors? You may open the right one or the left.

Ali:
Am I allowed to have a look first, so that I know which suits me?

SPEECH	MUSIC

Guardian:
Certainly. Which would you see first?

Ali:
The Paradise of the bad men. I have never heard of it before.

Narrator:
The guardian opened the door

Decide on the type of door and appropriate sounds. What is it made of? Is it large or small? Start the sounds of the 'light-filled hall' music gradually and rise to a crescendo after this sentence.

and Ali found himself in a splendid hall full of light.

The smaller sounds of the 'light-filled hall' music can then be used below the speech.

In the centre stood a huge table decked in shimmering cloth and loaded with dish after dish of the most wonderful food.

The Food Music.

Around the table stood armchairs and on them sat the spirits of the dead. Each had his left hand tied to the arm of his chair and to his right arm was fixed a long, long spoon.

A descriptive sound for the spoon might be created, such as: two long scrapes on a scraper, followed by a metallic sound like a triangle.

The spoon was long enough to reach every one of the tempting dishes on the table. But it was much too long to be retracted to the hungry mouth.
Thus the hall was filled with sighs of frustration and desperate complaints.

The music of the Discontented Spirits starts gradually.

Ali:
(screams) No! That is not my idea of Paradise! May I please see the other place?

An angry version of the Ali tune.

Narrator:
The guardian opened the right door. And again Ali found himself in a wide shiny hall full of light. In the centre stood the table decked in spotless cloth and it was covered in a multitude of plates and dishes filled with wonderful food. Around stood the armchairs. On the chairs sat the spirits of the dead. And each of them had his left hand tied to the chair and the right to a long, long spoon. But instead of trying to bring the spoon to his own mouth—which he couldn't—everyone was feeding his opposite neighbour. And the hall was filled with gay laughter and happiness.

Repeat music as before.

The music of the Happy Spirits starts and grows gradually.

SUGGESTIONS FOR FURTHER READING

Addison, Richard, *Bright Ideas: Music* (Scholastic, Leamington Spa, 1987) ISBN 0 59070 700 0

Chatterley, Albert, *The Music Club Book* (Stainer & Bell, London, 1978) ISBN 0 85249 497 1

Davies, L., *Sound Waves* (Harper Collins Educational, London, 1985) ISBN 0 00312 529 7

Gilbert, J., *Story, Song and Dance* (Cambridge University Press, Cambridge, 1990) ISBN 0 52133 967 7

Glazer, Jo & Ward, Stephen, *Teaching Music in the Primary School* (Cassell, London, 1993) ISBN 0 30432 598 8 (hardback) 0 30432 578 3 (paperback)

Mills, Janet, *Music in the Primary School* (Cambridge University Press, Cambridge, 1991) ISBN 0 52144 825 5

Paynter, John, *Sound and Structure* (Cambridge University Press, Cambridge, 1992) ISBN 0 52135 581 8 (hardback) 0 52135 676 8 (paperback)

Schafer, Murray, *The Thinking Ear* (Arcana, Canada, 1986)

Swanich, K. and Tillman, June B., 'A Sequence of Musical Development: A Study of Children's Composition', *British Journal of Music Education*, Vol. 3, No. 3, pp. 305–339 (1986)

Tillman, June B., (ed.), *The Christmas Search* (Cambridge University Press, Cambridge, 1990) ISBN 0 52133 968 5

Tillman, June B. and Braley, Bernard (eds.), *New Horizons* (Stainer & Bell, London 1974) ISBN 0 85249 286 3

York, Mary, *Gently into Music* (Longman, Harlow, 1988) ISBN 0 58218 673 0. Cassette also available: ISBN 0 58218 672 2

INDEX

99

102